KISS AND TELL

Restoration Comedy of Manners:
Monologues, Scenes and Historical Context

Smith and Kraus *Books For Actors*

THE MONOLOGUE SERIES
> The Best Men's Stage Monologues of 1992
> The Best Women's Stage Monologues of 1992
> The Best Men's Stage Monologues of 1991
> The Best Women's Stage Monologues of 1991
> The Best Men's Stage Monologues of 1990
> The Best Women's Stage Monologues of 1990
> One Hundred Men's Stage Monologues from the 1980's
> One Hundred Women's Stage Monologues from the 1980's
> Street Talk: Character Monologues for Actors
> Uptown: Character Monologues for Actors
> Monologues from Contemporary Literature: Volume I
> Monologues from Classic Plays

FESTIVAL MONOLOGUE SERIES
> The Great Monologues from the Humana Festival
> The Great Monologues from the EST Marathon
> The Great Monologues from the Women's Project
> The Great Monologues from the Mark Taper Forum

YOUNG ACTORS SERIES
> Great Scenes and Monologues for Children
> New Plays from A.C.T.'s Young Conservatory
> Great Scenes for Young Actors from the Stage
> Great Monologues for Young Actors

SCENE STUDY SERIES
> The Best Stage Scenes of 1992
> The Best Stage Scenes for Women from the 1980's
> The Best Stage Scenes for Men from the 1980's

PLAYS FOR ACTORS SERIES
> Seventeen Short Plays by Romulus Linney
> Eric Overmyer: Collected Plays
> Lanford Wilson: 21 Short Plays
> William Mastrosimone: Collected Plays
> Terrence McNally: Collected Plays

GREAT TRANSLATION FOR ACTORS SERIES
> The Wood Demon by Anton Chekhov

OTHER BOOKS IN OUR COLLECTION
> Humana Festival '93: The Complete Plays
> The Actor's Chekhov
> Women Playwrights: The Best Plays of 1992

If you require pre-publication information about upcoming Smith and Kraus monologues collections, scene collections, play anthologies, advanced acting books, and books for young actors, you may receive our semi-annual catalogue, free of charge, by sending your name and address to **Smith and Kraus Catalogue, P.O. Box 10, Newbury, VT 05051. (800) 862 5423 FAX (802) 866 5346**

 KISS AND TELL

Restoration Comedy of Manners:
Monologues, Scenes and Historical Context

Edited by Michael Bigelow Dixon & Michele Volansky

SK
A Smith and Kraus Book

Kiss and Tell: Restoration Monologues, Scenes and Historical Context

A Smith and Kraus Book
Published by Smith and Kraus, Inc.
Newbury, Vermont
Copyright © 1993 by Smith and Kraus, Inc.
All rights reserved

COVER AND TEXT DESIGN BY JULIA HILL
Manufactured in the United States of America

First Edition: August 1993
10 9 8 7 6 5 4 3 2 1

Cover Illustration: William Hogarth's *Before*. Courtesy of the Print Collection, Lewis Walpole Library, Yale University.

Library of Congress Cataloging–In–Publication Data

Kiss and tell: Restoration comedy of manners : scenes, monologues and historical
    context / edited by Michael Bigelow Dixon and Michele Volansky.
    — 1st ed.
        p. cm.
    Includes bibliographical references.
    ISBN 1-880399-38-5 $11.95
    1. Acting. 2. Monologues. 3. English drama — Restoration, 1660-1700.
    4. English drama (comedy) I. Dixon, Michael Bigelow. II. Volansky,
    Michele.
    PN2080.K52 1993
    822'.0450817—dc20
                    93-30433
                    CIP

The editors
wish to thank
the following persons
for their dramaturgical expertise
and their assistance
in compiling the material
in this volume:

Liz Engelman
Jon Jory
David Kuntz
Sandee McGlaun
Aimee Michel
Amy Smith
Val Smith
Lisa Timmel
Jim Valone
Scott Zigler

Contents

SCENES

SCENES FOR TWO MEN

SCENES FOR TWO WOMEN

SCENES FOR ONE WOMAN AND ONE MAN

SOURCES

SELECTED BIBLIOGRAPHY

PREFACE

Michael Bigelow Dixon & Michele Volansky

Restoration theatre – like the weather – is a subject people talk of but no one does much about. How many Restoration plays have you seen on stage in America? Not many, most likely, which is too bad, since the Restoration Comedy of Manners is a vivid, scintillant, rapacious genre that harbors remarkable parallels to the ongoing battle between the sexes at the end of the 20th century.

The reasons for *not* producing plays from the Restoration era (1660 – circa 1710) are plentiful: the costumes and wigs are expensive, the loosely-plotted conflicts seem too contrived or convoluted for a modern audience, and the language makes huge technical demands on "Method" actors. Thankfully, Restoration plays are taught at universities, where the period is proclaimed the second flowering of the English stage, and occasionally a university theatre will tackle a production. But professional companies eschew the Restoration era like the plague it suffered from, which is a loss for contemporary audiences and actors who would enjoy this scandalous and scampish comedy.

Given all the festivals in America dedicated to Shakespeare, it's surprising that some theatre somewhere hasn't revived with regularity plays from the Restoration, even with their inherent difficulties. That loophole in our repertoire is one reason Actors Theatre of Louisville Producing Director Jon Jory selected Restoration Comedy of Manners as the topic for the theatre's 1992 Classics in Context Festival. This vôlume is a fortuitous by-product of that Festival, which contextualized productions of George Farquhar's *The Beaux' Strategem* and an adaptation of John Aubrey's *Brief Lives* with a series of lectures, films, panel discussions, exhibits and events. (The program for that Classics in Context Festival follows.) One of those events was an evening of monologues excerpted from various Restoration comedies. Entitled *Kiss and Tell*, that performance collage was acted by the Actors Theatre of Louisville apprentice company and directed by Scott Zigler and Aimee Michel.

Though we anticipated a relatively small turnout for what we felt might be a fairly esoteric Festival, the Restoration Comedy of

Manners proved popular with theatre professionals, scholars and the general public. A small printing of the collected *Kiss and Tell* monologues sold out immediately at the Festival bookshop, confirming our growing suspicion that there is, in fact, a real hunger for the glittering wit and power politics on display in Restoration comedy. To further whet that appetite, we have compiled this anthology of scenes and monologues – a collection replete with intrigue, manipulation and romance. Furthermore, the historical articles by Albert Wertheim and Judith Milhous offer fascinating background to the plays and provide invaluable clues to the performance style and meaning of Restoration comedy.

If the scenes and monologues interest, by all means search out and read the plays listed in the back. If a play interests, by all means encourage a theatre to produce it. Yes, the material is demanding. The ideas need to be thought through and driven home, and the sophisticated language requires nuance and passion. Yet when actors and directors bring these words to life, the plays slash and sparkle with their own amazing, albeit eccentric, vitality.

Michael Bigelow Dixon is the literary manager and dramaturg at Actors Theatre of Louisville where he researches and advises on the annual Humana Festival of New American Plays, Classics in Context Festival, and Flying Solo/Festival of Solo Performance. He has edited several volumes of new plays from Actors Theatre, and has written more than twenty plays that have been produced, published and/or televised. He was a Fellow at the National Endowment for the Arts, and has taught at North Carolina Central University, Rice University, and the University of California, Riverside.

Michele Volansky is the assistant literary manager and a dramaturg at Actors Theatre of Louisville, where she works on the annual Humana Festival of New American Plays and the Classics in Context Festival. She served as dramaturg for *Kiss and Tell* and provided educational materials on the Restoration Classics in Context Festival for Lousiville-area schools. She has dramaturged productions at Villanova University, Swarthmore College, Philadelphia Theatre Company and Atlantic Theatre Company, and has directed for high school and college students. She holds a Master's degree in Theatre/Dramaturgy from Villanova University.

ACTORS THEATRE OF LOUISVILLE
Classics in Context

The Classics in Context Festival is a month-long, multi-disciplinary event that revitalizes dramatic literature's masterworks for today's audience by examining the social, political and aesthetic influences surrounding the creation of the plays. Actors Theatre of Louisville uses plays as the centerpiece of the Festival, adding support events that include lectures, films, exhibits, and discussions. Actors Theatre's Producing Director Jon Jory originated Classics in Context in 1985, and Restoration Comedy of Manners was the focus of the 1992 Festival. The events from that Festival are listed below:

COMEDY OF MANNERS:
THE RESTORATION AND EARLY 18TH CENTURY

PERFORMANCES
The Beaux' Stratagem by George Farquhar, directed by Jon Jory
Brief Lives by John Aubrey, adapted by Patrick Garland, directed by Ray Fry
Kiss and Tell, directed by Scott Zigler and Aimee Michel
VIDEO
The Country Wife by William Wycherly, Stratford Festival production
    directed by John Cotterell, video directed by John Thomas.
LECTURES
Restoration Drama: The Second Flowering of the English Theatre, by Albert
    Wertheim
Charles' Fountain, The Pineapple, and the Oyster Woman: Theatricality,
Libertinism, and Politics in the Mirror of the Crown, by Julie Stone Peters
Aphra Behn's Novel - OROONOKO, by Linda Kerr Norflett
Henry Purcell's Opera - DIDO AND AENEAS, by Thomson Smillie
COLLOQUIA
Theatre Censorship: The Collier Controversy Revisited, with Joe Roach,
    Laurence Senelick and Ben Cameron
Women on Stage/Women in Society, with Judith Milhouse, Deborah Payne and
    Patricia Troxel.
EXHIBITS
Elegant Habits: Fashion of the Restoration, curated by Marcia Dixcy
Bigwigs of the Restoration and Early Augustan Age
SCHOLARS IN RESIDENCE
Jim Valone, Bellarmine College
Linda Kerr Norflett, North Carolina Central University

RESTORATION DRAMA:

The Second Flowering of the the English Theatre ✒
by Albert Wertheim

Pivotal for understanding both the emergence of England as a world power and to this day perhaps the world's greatest theatre-producing nation are the radical political events and social changes England experienced during the seventeenth-century. Under Queen Elizabeth and her successor James I, England flourished as never before. Once seen as an island nation of minor importance in comparison to such powers as France, Italy, and Spain, England, after the defeat of the Spanish Armada, emerged as a naval power whose fleets could protect England from foreign invasion and also could enable the English to invest in the New World by sending out explorers and potential settlers. With the smooth transfer of government from Elizabeth, the virgin Tudor queen, to a Scottish Stuart king, James, who agreed to become a Protestant when he assumed the English throne and who authorized the Protestant King James version of the Bible to prove his new religious allegiance, England was a nation with its religious problems settled and with the Church of England as its established religion. And under Queen Elizabeth and her Stuart successors, England and more especially London became a center for the arts, and in particular theatre. During the reign of James I, however, a Puritan counter-culture began to build up, and with the reign of Charles I, James' rather overrefined and ineffective son, the Puritans gained the upper hand until they at last deposed the king and took over the government. In the world of theatre, the great age of Shakespeare and Elizabethan drama officially came to an end in 1642, the year the English Puritans, under the leadership of Oliver Cromwell, ousted Charles, whom they later beheaded. The Puritans were to capture the government of England for the next eighteen years. In the years from 1642 to 1660, the Puritans, led by Cromwell, waged war on two fronts: they battled against the Loyalist forces led by Prince Charles, Charles I's son and legal heir to the English throne; and they fought against both secular and religious art, which they considered the work of the devil. They smashed the stained glass windows of churches and destroyed the ornaments on buildings, and demolished those bastions of licentiousness, the theatres. The playhouses, which had been built for the works of Shakespeare and his successors were relentlessly torn down by dint of Puritans zeal, playwrights went into early retirement, and actors found other jobs. More important, the spirit of Elizabethan drama was largely extinguished, playwriting essentially came to an end, and new actors, who in Shakespeare's day had been exclusively men, were no longer being trained.

In 1660, after eighteen years of bitter struggle, the Loyalists defeated the Puritans and the kings of England returned once more to power. On May 29, 1660, on his thirtieth birthday, the newly anointed King Charles II rode triumphantly through the streets of London to Whitehall, the ancestral palace of the kings of England, and initiated what is commonly called the Restoration Age because monarchy, the Parliament and the Church of England were once and for all *restored*.

Every action, it seems, has its equal and opposite reaction in art and life as well as in physics. Thus, the Puritan austerity of lifestyle and hatred of art that characterized the so-called interregnum period from 1642 to 1660 were swept aside and replaced by an era of strong kingship, sexual freedom among the aristocracy and a renewed interest in the arts, especially in theatre, acting and playwriting.

In August, 1660, less than three months after Charles II returned to his throne, he licensed two new theatre companies, the King's Company and the Duke's Company. These were to be the only legal theatres in London, and hence the birth of terms that remain to this day: *licensed theatres* and *legitimate theatres*. First putting on plays in several makeshift buildings, the King's Company finally took up permanent residency in the first of many theatres to be called Drury Lane. The Duke's Company was first housed in a converted tennis court, the Lincoln's Inn Fields Theatre, until they moved in 1671 to the building expressly constructed for them with elaborate scenic capacity, the Dorset Garden Theatre. In the playhouses built expressly for them, the two new legitimate theatre companies were granted a virtual monopoly over theatre in London, and they quickly began work by first rounding up older actors who had survived the war against the Puritans to have them revive old plays by Shakespeare and his contemporaries.

Two men, Thomas Killigrew and Sir William Davenant, who had been budding young playwrights in the late 1630s and whose playwriting careers had been prematurely curtailed by the Puritans, became the heads of the two new licensed rival acting companies. This gave them extraordinary power, and for many years these two men singlehandedly determined the course of Restoration drama. Killigrew's and Davenant's mandate from the King was to restore again to England the theatre life that had flourished during the first three decades of the seventeenth century. Their work cut out for them, they addressed the task of once more encouraging playwriting, bringing audiences back into playhouses, and finding actors who could perform in both new plays and revivals of old ones.

With no new actors having been trained for eighteen years, getting theatre back on its feet was no easy assignment. In Shakespeare's day, the roles of women had been played by highly and professionally trained boy actors; but no boy actors had been trained since the 1630s and these were all now grown men. The English theatres thus for the first time in history witnessed females, actresses, treading their boards. Actresses had long been used abroad, and indeed many of the British aristocracy who had lived in exile in France during the war years had seen women acting in the French theatre and had recognized the special attractions and attractiveness of seeing female performers on stage. Although bringing actresses to the stage was clearly an expedient measure for getting the theatre back on its feet, it was also a slap in the face for the defeated Puritans for whom women on stage would have been anathema. The actresses were not the only thing new in the Restoration theatre, for the two acting companies, though reviving Shakespeare and other Elizabethan playwrights, consciously sought not to return to the drama of an earlier day but to develop an entirely new theatre both in form and content. The public playhouses of earlier days, like Shakespeare's Globe, were timber buildings housing perhaps 3,000 spectators, 2,000 of whom were groundlings who stood without a roof over them in front of the stage, and a 1,000 others paid a higher admission fee to be seated in roofed galleries. The two new Restoration playhouses, by contrast, were built of timber and brick, were entirely roofed, and held an audience of 500. In Covent Garden and Drury Lane there were no standing groundlings. Indeed, there were no standees at all: everyone sat. The theatres were divided into three seating areas: box, pit, and galleries. In the boxes, which were at the back of the theatre and ran along the sides up to the stage and which cost 4 shillings, were seated the affluent and fashionable ladies and gentlemen; the gentry sat in the pit for 2 shillings sixpence; the middle class paid 1 shilling sixpence to sit in the main gallery; and servants and apprentices, who paid 1 shilling, occupied the upper gallery. Since no seats were reserved, more affluent patrons might send their servants to wait in line and hold a good seat for them. A new play at a Restoration theatre usually ran for three days. The proceeds from the first two days went to the actors and other theatre personnel. The take from the third performance was for the benefit of the playwright; and hence the term a "benefit performance."

Shakespeare's stage had been an open, thrust stage, a stage that jutted out into the audience. The Restoration playhouses introduced what is sometimes called a "picture stage," behind a curtain that was opened and that hung from an ornately carved and decorated gilt proscenium arch. A substantial forestage was placed in front of the proscenium arch and there was a rather large main stage behind it. Musicians in the Elizabethan theatre probably were located in an upper gallery above the stage. The Restoration stage may have inaugurated the orchestra pit, an area under the large forestage, a concept that is still with us in the contemporary theatre. At right angles to the proscenium arch and on either side of it were two large forestage doors wide enough to admit not merely actors but coaches and in some productions even horses. Those doors could also be used to represent the door to houses or closets where characters could hide.

Shakespeare's plays were given in the afternoon and lit by the daylight that shone in upon the mostly roofless theatre. Placed in a roofed building, the Restoration stage was lit by candles placed in chandeliers and eventually by oil lamps that served as footlights. Whereas Shakespeare's plays had been performed on a bare stage without sets, the Restoration theatres had four spaced pairs of wing flats or shutters that were placed in grooves and could be pushed together to form painted backdrops for a scene, and that could be pulled apart or opened to reveal subsequent scenes. When we nowadays speak metaphorically about "the scene opens" or "the scene closes," we should know that those metaphors are based on the very real facts of Restoration theatre when scenes literally opened and closed. Those scenes were often elaborately painted and might depict forests, gardens, battlefields, bedrooms, London streets, or ale houses.

The theatre of Shakespeare's day used only the barest of props: a dagger for Macbeth, a chalice for Hamlet's mother, a letter for Beatrice and Benedick. The Restoration theatre, however, had substantial props like trees, dressing tables, and battlements. Actors might sit on chairs or be found lying in beds. And with the development of theatre technology on the Continent, the Restoration playhouses were increasingly equipped with an arsenal of machinery for technical effects. Characters could, for example, descend on cloud machines or be seen on boats seemingly crossing tempestuous water.

Restoration plays, which were often about contemporary society, were performed by actors and actresses in fashionable clothes. For the actresses that might mean dresses with extensive decolletage and skirts with many petticoats; for the actors it meant periwigs, broad-brimmed hats, waistcoats with floral designs, cravats of lace, shoes and stockings. Exotic costumes were available for the many Restoration tragedies and heroic plays set in foreign climes. Since boxes for fashionable ladies and gentlemen flanked the forestage, it was the case that in Restoration comedies, which usually dealt with the contemporary scene, actors and actresses on stage would be dressed like the largely aristocratic audience alongside them in the boxes. The social and often satiric relevance of the plays would thus often be immediately and visually apparent. Indeed it was often the case that the very social figures being spoofed in a play would actually be present in a box right next to the action.

The demeanor of the audience at a Restoration theatre was very different from a modern audience. Today, when a play begins, all become quiet and attentive. Not so at a Restoration playhouse, where one often went more to see and be seen than to attend the play. There were, of course, theatre aficionados like the diarist Samuel Pepys, who complained bitterly about the unruliness of the audience, for a play to many was merely an occasion to meet friends, gossip, argue, sport new clothes, make loud witty or witless comments about the play one was only half listening to, or arrange an after-theatre rendezvous with a mistress or a prostitute. Even as a play was going on, orange women were selling their refreshments to inattentive spectators. A close modern equivalent to audience behavior at a Restoration play is the behavior of spectators at a college football game, which is attended as much as a social occasion as a sporting event. At the football games as at a Restoration play, spectators often watch the action half-heartedly while their attention is directed more squarely on meeting and chatting with old friends, cutting a figure in new clothes of the fall season, or drinking. Only at the critical moments when goals are scored are all eyes and attention actually riveted on the playing field. At the two Restoration theatres, admission was charged only after the third act. Since Dorset Garden and Drury Lane were very close to one another, one might attend the first acts at one theatre to see who was there and then hop over to the other to see if the audience there was more interesting. Writing for the Restoration theatre was clearly a real challenge for any playwright, for the characters, action and drama on stage would have that going on in the boxes, pit and galleries in front of the stage.

Killigrew's King's Company had many of the old actors including two famous ones, Michael Mohun and Charles Hart. Davenant's Duke's Company featured the leading young actor of the day, Thomas Betterton, who is one of the England's great actors in the annals of English drama. The actors working in the new Restoration theatres sometimes proved to be a problem, for many of them were frequently in debt and others were well known as drunkards and debauchees. Worse yet were the new actresses, a number of whom had taken up a theatrical career because it provided an opportunity for them to meet a rich lord whose kept mistress they might become. Of course the greatest example of this was the actress Nell Gwynn, who became the most famous of King Charles II's mistresses. Since everybody seemed to know everybody else's scandalous secrets, sexually active actresses were often laughed at when they played the roles of put upon virgins. The famous actress Mrs. Barry, for example, was the mistress of the notoriously licentious Earl of Rochester; and once in a tragedy when she had to exclaim about her "virgin innocence," she brought the house down with laughter.

The playhouses and the players, the costumes, props and sets of the new Restoration theatre were not the only novelties. The plays themselves were very different from the ones at the beginning of the century when Shakespeare, Marlowe, Ben Jonson, Beaumont and Fletcher, and Thomas Heywood and Thomas Middleton were the leading dramatists of the day and held sway over the dramatic tastes of the time. Since many of the Restoration playwrights had been in exile in France during the Puritan days, they had supplemented their knowledge of Elizabethan English drama with the French dramas of Corneille, Racine, and most especially Moliere. Drawing on the two traditions, British and French, the new playwrights who emerged after 1660 ushered in an era of English theatre that did not imitate but came to rival the preceding Elizabethan age.

Serious theatre in the Restoration was dominated by heroic tragedy usually written in rhymed couplets, populated by extraordinarily exotic heroes and heroines, and contained highly improbable and operatic plots that centered on the problems of love and honor or love versus honor. More memorable and more successful than the serious plays were the comic ones, most of which were written in the style of what has come to be known as Restoration "comedy of manners." The term "comedy of manners" is a loose and tricky one that seems to take on somewhat different dimensions and emphases with every critic who discusses it. Certainly manners comedy was not an invention of the Restoration theatre, but it did characterize most of the comic plays written for the English stage during the sixty years from 1660 until the third decade of the eighteenth century. Although almost every comic playwright writing during that period attempted to write brilliant and brilliantly witty comedies of manners, none had the eclat and success of the "big five," the five comic dramatists whose panache and wit mark them as the major writers of the period. Those five remarkable playwrights are Sir George Etherege, most remembered for his *The Man of Mode* or *Sir Fopling Flutter* (1676); William Wycherley, whose *The Country Wife* (1675) and *The Plain Dealer* (1676) continue to be frequently revived; William Congreve, who wrote *Love for Love* (1695) and whose *The Way of the World* (1700) is often considered the high water mark of Restoration comedy of manners; Sir John Vanbrugh,who as an architect designed Castle Howard and Blenheim Palace, and who as a playwright is most remembered for *The Relapse* (1696) and *The Provok'd Wife* (1697); and George Farquhar, whose wonderful comedy *The Beaux' Stratagem* (1707) continues to be the most popular, beloved and stageworthy play of the period. None of these men were prolific writers, however. The mainstays of the theatre were such playwrights as John Dryden, Aphra Behn, Thomas Durfey, and Edward Ravenscroft.

For the most part, comedy of manners focuses on the foibles and comic idiosyncrasies of a particular social world and its social rules. At the heart of most comedies of manners is a central couple who represent all the sparkle and social finesse of the beautiful fashionable world, the *beau monde*. They tend to be masters of language and of verbal wit or repartee, they know how to dress in tune with current fashions without over-dressing, they can master their feelings and passions so that they are not mastered by them, and they know how to play the games of sex and marriage so brilliantly that they do not get caught out. Around the central couple circle the less socially adroit who are satirized to the degree that they fall short of social brilliance. The broadest targets of satire are the bumpkins, the foreigners, and the fops. Since the point of view in the comedy of manners tends to be an urban one, there is much laughter at the expense of those who come to London from the country and whose manners are necessarily gauche and unknowing. Wit in the city belongs to an "in" crowd, and no one is more out of it than a man bred in the provinces who does not know how to tie a cravat, perfume himself with orange water, or make a sexual assignation with a possible mistress. Not knowing the way of the world in London, the bucolics either make asses of themselves or become literally and metaphorically drunk on the strong potations of the town. The satire is directed at their foibles and shortcomings, and that satire simultaneously sets into relief and italicizes the contrasting aplomb of the worldly wise hero and heroine. Similarly, the comedy of manners frequently includes foreigners who have mastered neither London's social rules nor the English language. But the sharpest satire is leveled at the fops, those dandies who are convinced they are masters of fashion but who lack the wit, the intelligence, to be anything more than overdressed, pretentious clothes horses. They appear on stage in overdone wigs and clothes that are so extreme in their would-be fashion consciousness that they are laughable. For the fops, who are all show and no intelligence, the comedy of manners reserves its nastiest barbs and its most extreme comic punishments.

Among the other characters of the plays, there are women who show their sexual proclivities too much or exhibit a meanness of spirit; and there are men who are either too calculating or too randy by half. Sexuality and shrewdness, especially in combination, are very much virtues in the comedy of manners, but only when they are kept covert, discreet and controlled behind a smokescreen of witty repartee, politeness and politesse.

Behind the examination of the way characters do or do not handle well the social graces or how they do or do not show true understanding of the manners of the town is an implicit sexual scenario. Consciously overturning the sexual prohibitions with which the Puritans sought to imbue English society, the court circle and aristocracy, who set the agendas of the Restoration period, fostered an age of fairly open sexual freedom hitherto unknown in England. Judging from many of the plays and much of the poetry of the period, mistresses, extra-marital and premarital affairs, corruption of other men's wives, oral and anal sex, and homosexuality were tolerated and in some cases practiced fairly openly. When Etherege has characters named Mrs. Loveit and Lady Cockwood, when Wycherley's hero is called Horner, and when Congreve's randy older matron is called Lady Wishfort, we need little help in understanding the sexual puns. But more than salacious punning is at work, for manners comedy uses the social world as a barometer for other things; so that the way the characters handle themselves in the "beau monde", in the social world, is the way that they will also handle themselves in bed. The Loveits and Cockwoods will be sexually insatiable but not giving. The fops like Etherege's Sir Fopling Flutter or Vanbrugh's Sir Novelty Fashion are likely to be all foreplay and likely impotent when push comes to shove. In some cases there are suggestions of homosexuality in the effeminacy of the fops. But the central paired characters, the characters of brilliant repartee, elegant but not overstated dress, and social eclat, Congreve's Mirabell and Millamant or his Valentine and Angelica, or Farquhar's Aimwell and Dorinda, these are the ones who by implication will achieve mutuality in their sexual congress and true satisfaction in bed. In other words, the comedy of manners while explicitly about social performance tends also implicitly to be about sexual performance.

In general, it is important to understand that the comedy of manners is about suave and gauche behavior in society and about what those behaviors imply about intelligence. It is a dramatic form populated by fools and fops, lusty matrons, jealous husbands, and brilliantly witty, highly polished aristocratic ladies and gentlemen. Its mainstay is the dialogue of wit and of wit combats. What Restoration manners comedy is not is a drama in which plot matters very much. Sometimes, as in Congreve's *The Way of the World*, the plot is so tangled that it is somewhere between difficult and impossible to follow. But the plot tends not to matter very much, for it is just a relatively unimportant framework for the presentation of sparkling dialogue and social types. To look for carefully constructed plots and the delivery of great philosophical ideas or truths in Restoration comedy is to miss completely what makes the theatre of Etherege, Wycherley, Congreve, Vanbrugh and Farquhar tick.

In a discussion of Restoration comedy of manners it would be amiss not to point out that it is largely a male driven, some would say male sexist, comedy; and that most often the main male character is very far from being a virtuous, true-blue, boy scout. He is, in fact, usually just the opposite: a rake, a libertine, a roue, a debaucher of women: in short, a Machiavel placed in the social milieu of polished society and replacing Machiavelli's political battles with the battles of the sexes. The libertine heroes in plays, moreover, are not dramatic concoctions but replications of the licentious males who populated and even dominated the court circle, and who were known as The Court Wits.

Libertinism on stage and off, furthermore, had a very real basis in contemporary Restoration philosophy or at least in a willful and skewed reading of that philosophy. In 1651, the famous English philosopher Thomas Hobbes published his *magnum opus*, *Leviathan*, in which he argued that reason is an immediate function of sense perception and not something that exists as a separate entity apart from the senses. Reasoning is, therefore, simply adding up our sense perceptions; and the only things that exist are the things we know through our senses. Consequently, it can be argued that God or Divine Spirit, which is not something we know through our senses, does not really exist. If we can argue that religion and ethics, which are not acquired through the senses are shams, and if we can agree that there is little evidence for an afterlife, then it is a short step to condoning libertinism or a life driven by the senses. If reason is a product of the senses, then the philosophical good must lie in following the senses to the fullest. That would be the most "reasonable" thing to do. Seen this way, a *carpe diem* philosophy of hedonism and libertinism is condoned; and promises, contracts, commitments, or lovers' vows, all of which do not derive from the senses, are invalid. This is a twisting of Hobbes but nonetheless a philosophical justification for the sexually aggressive and sometimes ruthless men who are presented as admirable heroes in Restoration comedy of manners.

By the end of the seventeenth century, a reaction to the sexual freedom of the age and to the sexual freedom presented in the theatre was setting in. In part this stems from the rise of a new English middle class and a changing theatre audience. The end of the century witnessed the emergence of a merchant class whose income was based on investments, often in the New World, and whose riches were beginning to out-distance those of the landed gentry, whose incomes were based on the more stable but less profitable ownership of land and on the rental income derived therefrom. The emerging merchant class, though no Puritans, consisted not of court wits who enjoyed the sexual license that came with aristocratic privilege, but of Mr. and Mrs. Middleclass Majority with parvenu and fairly moral attitudes. A measure of the changing moral climate came in 1698 with Jeremy Collier's now famous *A Short View of the Immorality and Profaneness of the English Stage*, a frontal attack on the theatre in which Collier blasted Restoration playwrights, plays, playhouses and performers for debauching audiences and the English citizenry. He deplored in strongest possible terms the libertinism and immodesty presented on stage and in dialogue, the abuse of holy scripture, the mockery of clergy, the implied approval of loose men and women, and the theatre's general encouragement of sexual appetite. Immoderate though it was, Collier's attack bespoke the winds of moral change and an increasing impatience with the sexual outspokenness of Restoration manners comedy. Although Collier's vituperation closed no theatres, there is no doubt that it had an effect upon the dramas that followed. And one of those dramas was George Farquhar's *The Beaux' Stratagem*, which opened in London in 1707 a few weeks before the playwright's death.

The last of the great comic playwrights of the Restoration, George Farquhar like so many other talented "English" writers was actually Irish. Here he falls in a class with Jonathan Swift, Richard Steele, Oscar Wilde, George Bernard Shaw, Samuel Beckett, Sir Richard Steele, and fellow playwright William Congreve. Born in Londonderry in 1677 or 1678, Farquhar was the son of an Anglican clergyman. He studied at Trinity College, Dublin; and in Dublin tried his hand with little success at an acting career. He did, however, become the friend of one of the most famous actors of the period, Robert Wilks, who had seen a sketch by Farquhar for a proposed play called *Love and a Bottle* and thereupon advised young Farquhar to give up acting, travel to London, and try his hand at playwriting. Farquhar followed Wilks' good advice, and in 1698, *Love and a Bottle* opened with modest success at Drury Lane. Once in London and consorting with the men and women of the theatre, Farquhar came to understand what sort of plays were likely to succeed on the London stage. The result was that in 1699, he scored a great hit with *The Constant Couple*, sometimes known as *The Trip to the Jubilee*. So popular was *The Constant Couple* that two years later Farquhar's sequel to it, *Sir Harry Wildair*, opened at Drury Lane. These successes were followed by less successful plays and, more important, by a disastrous marriage in 1703 to Margaret Pemell, a widow with two children and with absolutely no money. Pemell seems to have tricked the playwright into marriage by pursuing him relentlessly, suggesting that she was an heiress, and not telling him of her severe poverty. Once married, Farquhar found that he had been deceived and that he now had a wife and children to support with but little means to do so. The embitterment Farquhar must have felt and his dire financial straits play an important role in understanding the final phase of both his playwriting career and his life.

A year after his marriage and in an attempt at some solvency, Farquhar joined the army as a Lieutenant of Grenadiers. As part of his duties he was sent into the English midlands to recruit new soldiers. This work provided a modicum of income but more important provided matter for one of his two most famous plays, *The Recruiting Officer*, which opened in April 1706 and which was an overwhelming success. It continues so to this day. To anyone who knows Farquhar's comedy, it should come as no surprise that Bertolt Brecht was to adapt it more than two centuries later under the title *Pauken und Trompeten (Drums and Trumpets)*.

The profits from *The Recruiting Officer* enabled Farquhar to get out of the army. By that point, however, he had also fallen ill. In a last ditch effort to secure funds for his family to survive, Farquhar, from what might be considered his death bed, penned *The Beaux' Stratagem*, his final and most famous play, and the one on which his lasting reputation as one of the greatest English playwrights rests. Surely the subject of divorce, one almost never mentioned in English poetry, drama or fiction before *The Beaux' Stratagem*, must surely have been influenced by Farquhar's sorry ruminations on his own most lamentable marital state.

One of the things that makes Farquhar's *The Beaux' Stratagem* so interesting is the way it picks up and employs the several things we have been discussing. When Farquhar wrote his comedy, he likely knew he was dying, that this would be his last play, and that the money he made from it would be the inheritance he could leave to his family. A shrewd observer of the London theatre climate and the current tastes of theatre patrons, Farquhar deftly weaves together the urban traditions of Restoration comedy, the new morality rearing its head in the work of Jeremy Collier and others, and his own sorry experience in the marriage market. For the viewer of *The Beaux' Stratagem* an immediate indicator that Farquhar is pulling away from the milieu of classic Restoration comedy is that the play is, remarkably, not set among the beautiful and frequently amoral London socialites. Its setting is, instead, rural Lichfield; and the first scene opens not in a London coffee house or tavern populated with the chic gentlemen who might gather there but in a country inn, the hideaway of highwaymen, run by a roguish innkeeper and his pert but unpolished daughter.

In the plays of Wycherley or Congreve, the country people alight in the city with mud on their boots and rustic coarseness in their behavior. Farquhar thus neatly and importantly turns the tables and gets both his characters and his play out of the urban scene that was beginning to suffer from the accusations of the new eighteenth-century moralists. In *The Beaux' Stratagem*, there are two elegant and citified gents, Aimwell and Archer, dressed in their finery who alight, portmanteaux in hand, in the country. The two young blades are broke and, therefore, see the heartlessness of the town and of a society in which affluence equals acceptance:

AIMWELL. But did you observe poor Jack Generous in the Park last week?

ARCHER. Yes, with his autumnal periwig, shading his melancholy face, his coat older than anything bit its fashion, with one hand idle in his pocket, and with the other picking his useless teeth; and though the Mall was crowded with company, yet was poor Jack as single and solitary as a lion in a desert.

AIMWELL. And as much avoided, for no crime upon earth but the want of money.

The sentiment and sentimentality as well as the mildly moralist tone nicely show Farquhar cutting his dramatic cloth to the tastes of the times. And what comes through, too, is the impressive way Farquhar has of taking the experience of his own sudden poverty as the matter from which to weave a fabric for his play. One can see, too, Farquhar deftly pulling away from the implicit Hobbesian philosophy of previous Restoration manners comedies which suggested reason was merely the sum of the senses; for Farquhar has Archer exclaim, "Give me a man that keeps his five senses keen and bright as his sword, that has 'em always drawn out in their just order and strength, with his reason as commander at the head of 'em." Here suddenly Reason is not a product of the senses but a separate entity meant to command the senses. Clearly what Farquhar is cleverly registering in 1707 is England's transition from the Restoration age of sensuality to the eighteenth-century Age of Reason.

Despite his tacit acknowledgment of a new moral turn and of a new exaltation of Reason, Farquhar is nonetheless a talented writer of manners comedy, and *The Beaux' Stratagem* has, on the one hand, a pair of romantic lovers, Aimwell and Dorinda, whose prose is often on the border of poetry; and on the other hand has the more attractive, because more hard-bitten and worldly, lovers, Archer and Mrs. Sullen, whose scintillating repartee is reminiscent of the sparkling wit exchanged between the admirable central couples in the comedies of Etherege, Wycherley and Congreve. One of the best moments of dialogue in *The Beaux' Stratagem* occurs when Mrs. Sullen daydreams aloud about Archer, and then he suddenly emerges from his hiding place in her bedroom closet:

MRS. SULLEN. Why, then suppose him here, dressed like a

youthful, gay, and burning bridegroom, (*here* ARCHER *steals out of the closet.*) with tongue enchanting, eyes bewitching, knees imploring.–(*Turns a little o' one side and sees* ARCHER *in the posture she describes.*) – Ah!– (*Shrieks, and runs to the other side of the stage.*) Have my thoughts raised a spirit?– What are you, sir, a man or a devil?

ARCHER. (*rising*) A man, a man, madam.

MRS. SULLEN. How shall I be sure of it?

ARCHER. Madam, I'll give you demonstration this minute. (*Takes her hand.*)

MRS. SULLEN. What, sir! do you intend to be rude?

ARCHER. Yes, madam, if you please.

MRS. SULLEN. In the name of wonder, whence came ye?

ARCHER. From the skies, madam–I'm a Jupiter in love, and you shall be my Alcmena.

MRS. SULLEN. How came you in?

ARCHER. I flew in at the window, madam; and your cousin Cupid lent me his wings, and your sister Venus opened the casement.

MRS. SULLEN. I'm struck dumb with admiration!

ARCHER. And I–with wonder! (*Looks passionately at her.*)

This dialogue nicely captures the way Archer for each of Mrs. Sullen's lines never misses a beat and has intelligent, clever, and even classical ripostes complete with sexual innuendo appropriate to the moment. It is such dialogue and the physical communication accompanying it that is at the heart of manners comedy in general and of Farquhar's *The Beaux' Stratagem* more particularly.

In the spirit of manners comedy, Farquhar also creates the character of the Frenchman, Bellair, who affords the playwright an occasion to satirize both foppishness and foreignness. Similarly, the false priest Foigard is drawn so that the play can hold both the Catholic clergy and the Irish peasantry up to ridicule. The silly Lady Bountiful, whose name has become a by-word in English, is gently ridiculed; and the sottish, boorish Sullen comes in for a major dose of scorn from both audience and dramatist. And Farquhar adds a unique element to the traditional hallmarks of manners comedy, for Farquhar had been reading the tracts on divorce written by, of all people, John Milton. Taking much of his matter from Milton's work, Farquhar raises the difficult question of divorce, something nearly impossible to obtain in his day, through his presentation of the disastrously matched Sullens. In this way, Farquhar adds an important and unusual serious political touch to what is otherwise a light and alternatingly romantic and roguish comedy.

The Beaux' Stratagem is one of the gems of the English dramatic repertoire. It was a smash hit when it was first performed, and it was revived over and over again in the eighteenth and nineteenth centuries. Even in our time it is among the most frequently performed English comedy of manners from the Restoration period. Farquhar's characters, language, and situations have enough of the universal in them to make his play enjoyable as meaningful theatre and not merely as a dramatic museum piece.

In the fifty-year period from 1660 to 1710, English drama experienced its second flowering. Although not, like the period of Elizabethan drama, graced by such literary giants as Shakespeare, Marlowe and Jonson, the Restoration was nonetheless an era in which major playwrights, particularly comic playwrights, lourished; and during which they presented their audiences then and now with sharply etched social caricatures and a sense of acceptable and unacceptable social behavior. The Restoration theatre, moreover, brought plays indoors, gave the audience seats, suggested the seating arrangement that still obtains in most playhouses, offered a life in the theatre to women, and made important strides in both set design and lighting. Most of all, it gave us a remarkable repertoire of plays that are actors' dreams and audience delights. It is a tribute to the genius of that period to say that The Beaux' Stratagem is not one of a kind but one of many wonderful plays we are privileged to have inherited from what was surely one of the world's most important ages of theatre.

Albert Wertheim is Associate Dean of the College of Arts and Sciences at Indiana University. He is Professor of English as well as Theatre and Drama and has taught at Princeton University. Professor Wertheim has published widely in the fields of Renaissance and Restoration drama, modern British and American drama, and Commonwealth literature. He has been the recipient of three distinguished teaching awards and fellowships at the Berkeley Repertory Theatre, The Folger Shakespeare Library, and the Newberry Library.

THE PROFESSION OF ACTING
IN LATE SEVENTEENTH-CENTURY LONDON ✍
by Judith Milhous

When the theatre re-opened in 1660, it did not seem to be short of people aspiring to become actors, but we have no direct testimony about what moved them to take up or renew this profession. How did someone become an actor, and what did it mean to join the profession? We have very little information about acting in specific English plays from the late seventeenth century. Daily newspapers did not exist; there were no reviews, no fan magazines, no instant biographies. No theatre building from the period survives in London. Although a few promptbooks have been preserved, most are for plays that were not successful, and in any case most of the annotations in them concern entrances and exits, scene changes, and music cues, rather than details of what happened onstage. Apart from the occasional anecdote, we are forced to generalize about acting in the period. Nevertheless, the general outlines of the profession are clear.

The first requirement for an actor is probably the right kind of personality, and the more acute observers of the age were aware that actors were different from other people in their demonstrativeness and lack of inhibition. The diarist Samuel Pepys describes a volatile new acquaintance as someone who could be an actor, that is, whose public presentation of himself commanded attention. Shrinking violets seldom last long on the stage.

Assuming the necessary exhibitionism was there, what else drew people to this career? Money was no doubt a factor, although most actors did not make a great deal of money. Each person presumably balanced the demands of the job against the small size of a beginner's salary. A theatre career offered the advantage of requiring brainwork rather than heavy physical labor. Acting presupposed literacy, which even in the metropolis would have ruled out many people. It provided relatively comfortable working conditions and a schedule with some flexibility. The extensive repertory built change into the job, a feature which might make it very attractive in comparison to a bureaucratic clerkship. The principal service position open to women, work as a companion, maid, or nurse, was both more demanding and less rewarding. On the other hand, theatre was not a respectable career in the eyes of the general populace, and it was not without its own limitations. We are probably safe in assuming that there was always a trickle of applicants, but seldom a flood, and we know that many who tried the stage did succeed. Yet, surprising as it seems to us, the theatre also offered a fair measure of security to many of its employees. The actor who fit into a company and earned a position was likely to keep it so long as he or she remained capable of doing the job.

The aspiring actor entered a system that was carefully regulated, both outside and inside. By law, there were at most two theatre companies in London, the King's Company and the Duke's Company. The actor who found no work at them "strolled" in the provinces or went to Ireland – or changed careers. Theatres were strictly commercial enterprises: no subsidies or grants cushioned their operation. At the beginning of the period they enjoyed extensive royal patronage, which made the theatre a fashionable place to be seen; but over the course of the next forty years that patronage declined to non-existence. The company that did not please its public and pay its tradesmen's bills went bankrupt. The King's Company averted that disaster only by amalgamating with the Duke's Company in 1682.

The theatre reflected the society at large in many ways, not least in its hierarchy and its sexism. A company consisted of several share-holding, senior male actors, who made all practical decisions, and a number of hirelings, who included the supporting men and all the women. This basic design was inherited from Elizabethan acting companies, which slotted boys into the category later filled by women. Seven or fewer actors shouldered the burden of all the leading roles, as well as management, and paid themselves accordingly. Principal actors held their positions essentially for life: this core shaped the entire generation that worked with them. Between 1660 and 1682, the chief man in charge of the King's Company were Charles Hart and Michael Mohun. For almost half a century after 1660, Thomas Betterton determined the shape of the Duke's Company he helped form in 1695. Anyone junior to these actors had to fit in around them. The majority of people who worked for any of these companies had no chance of rising to such exalted levels.

Below the principal actors, there were at least three salary levels among hirelings, and there were also unpaid positions. To deal with the latter first, the eighteenth-century actor-manager Colley Cibber provides a colorful story of his entrée into the United Company around 1690. He cultivated the prompter, buying him drinks, and was rewarded with a succession of unpaid walk-ons. Eventually he was entrusted with a line, which in his excitement he blew, thereby infuriating Thomas Betterton. When Betterton ordered Cibber fined, the prompter replied that Cibber was unpaid, and Betterton said, "Why then put him down ten shillings a week, and forfeit him 5s." That turns out to be the bottom of the scale for actors.

Many men began acting careers on their own initiative; how women were recruited is less clear. Like the boy actors they replaced, they were regarded as transients. Many applied out of economic necessity. Some came personally recommended by former keepers: Sir George Etherege, having seduced the fourteen-year-old Elizabeth Price, introduced her to the Duke's Company, but she did not flourish as an actress. No salary information is preserved for the theatre until the 1690's, but once it becomes available it shows that women were paid significantly less than men. Elizabeth Price's tastes ran to a more expensive life, and she left the theatre for a succession of keepers, eventually marrying an earl. The wonder is that any built careers inside the theatre.

In due course, theatrical families came to be a slightly more reliable source of performers, male and female. Three generations of the Leigh family graced the English stage, though in less and less distinguished ranks. Susanna Percival was the daughter of a minor actor and wife to two stars. She married first William Mountfort, and then John Verbruggen (after Mountfort was murdered by a teenaged nobleman bent on abducting another actress). Wives and daughters were subject to the legal control of husbands and fathers and less likely to stray than free agents. Nevertheless, the most dedicated and successful actresses of the period, Elizabeth Barry and Anne Bracegirdle, came from outside the theatre, and there were good reasons why they remained unmarried.

Most of the training a beginner received took place on the job, by observation and in a master-apprentice pattern which left no records. (Although an attempt was made in the 1670s to run a formal acting school, it did not work out.) Aspiring actors played many walk-ons, only gradually acquiring lines, as the Cibber example demonstrates. A hireling who showed enterprise and dependability could expect steady employment for the approximately 180 to 200 days of the theatre season. In that time the company would present between 40 and 60 plays, depending on the number and success of new productions. Although this schedule sounds brutal, for all but the top handful of actors, it was not that demanding. To point to familiar Shakespeare examples, Horatio may stand around a lot, but Hamlet has all the lines. Claudius and Laertes are much lighter roles, Gertrude and Ophelia lighter still, and any number of beginners could swell the court scenes. In some of Shakespeare's comedies one or two women have more substantial roles, but the men still outnumber and out-talk them. Plays written after 1660 give more stage time, but men remain more important and more numerous.

Since at least a third to a half of the plays in the repertory came round again year after year, an actor who lasted five or more seasons would soon have been familiar with most of the plays he or she would ever be in. The repertory is daunting at first sight, but less so for a permanent than for a temporary employee. It also offered the advantage of variety, both to the actors and to the audience. How much more interesting to cook – or eat – at a restaurant whose menu varies with what's in the market, than at one which always serves the same thing.

In this sort of company actors owned their own roles: not only did they literally hold onto the sides on which their lines were written, but for the sake of efficiency management expected that most of a cast would repeat whatever roles they were first assigned. To cite an example made extreme by seniority, Thomas Betterton played Amintor in *The Maid's Tragedy* and Hamlet, among other roles, for fifty years. Most supporting actors and women did not endure quite so long, though Elizabeth Barry lasted better than most, in no small part because she participated in the management of the rebel actors' company after 1695.

While actors certainly lobbied for roles in new plays or for roles vacated by death or resignation, there were no regular tryouts. In a sense, the hirelings tried out every time they went onstage, and most playwrights wrote with particular performers in mind. That means that an actor's range can be estimated by reading through his or her roles in order. Playwrights regarded some as quite limited, but offered others great variety. They also expected performers to fill out the characterization of formulaic roles. Without overstressing experiment, we can say that, within certain limits, creative acting was encouraged, though perhaps not demanded. Ben the Sailor in *Love for Love* functions as a callow youth and might have been little more. But Thomas Doggett researched the role by boarding among sailors along the waterfront in Wapping, and the unique details he added to what Congreve had written made him a rising star. (Shortly thereafter, he decided that he had rather lead a provincial company than be a subordinate in London.) At the end of the century, reformers in the audience wrote down dialogue to use against the actors in lawsuits charging them with profanity and blasphemy. As these transcriptions make clear, the letter of the text was far from sacred to hirelings, and the low comedians were especially prone to ad-libbing and embroidering on themes. Principal actors were on the whole more responsible about knowing their lines, and some, like Robert Wilks, were fanatically opposed to variations.

The endlessly-rotating but fairly stable repertory dictated a very different approach to rehearsals than we are used to. A new play got approximately a month's rehearsals, unless it involved complicated masque sequences. The author usually directed: he steeled questions of interpretation; set up the traffic patterns; and approved technical elements of the production. Scenery was pulled from stock for most plays, and no furniture appeared onstage unless the action required it. Actors were expected to learn their lines on their own, not during rehearsals. After a session or two spent exploring the script, most rehearsals were fairly low-key. After all, these people played opposite one another every day and knew one another's capabilities. They could walk through most rehearsals and not slight a production.

Duels and elaborate sequences of physical comedy were probably worked out privately among the actors involved, and again there is scope for as much imagination as a given team of actors cared to invest. Cibber reports of James Nokes and Tony Leigh in Thomas Otway's comedy, *The Souldier's Fortune*, that "they returned the Ball so dexterously upon one another, that every Scene between them seem'd but one continued Rest [i.e., tennis rally] of Excellence," and we have other reports of elaborate physical as well as verbal routines among comedians.

For a play being revived from the recent past, the leading actor usually served as director. Efficiency dictated that the revival conform to a previous pattern. This respect for the past, regardless of authenticity, was very strong. At the beginning of his career, Betterton was taught to play Hamlet "in every Particle" as it had been played by Shakespeare's company, though the only link was the fallible one of Sir William Davenant's memory. At the end of the century, when a minor actor recalled a particular line reading that Betterton was groping for in rehearsal of an old play, he was rewarded with a tip for remembering the "right" delivery.

Even though the pressures of business put a premium on consistency, there was room in the company for actors who depended on inspiration as well as for those who "studied" their parts. The original Oroonoko, John Verbruggen, was described by a nostalgic colleague as a quick study who "had the Words perfect at one View," after which, "Nature directed 'em into Voice and Action...His chief Parts were *Bajazet, Oroonoko, Edgar* in King *Lear, Wilmore* in the *Rover*, and *Cassius*, when Mr. *Betterton* play'd *Brutus* with him.–Then you might behold the grand Contest, *viz.* whether Nature or Art excell'd – *Verbruggen* wild and untaught, or *Betterton* in the Trammels of Instruction...Nature was so predominant [in Verbruggen], that his second Thoughts never alter'd his prime Performance." Likewise in *The Rover*, "never were more beautiful Scenes than between him, and Mrs. *Bracegirdle*, in the Character of *Helena*; for, what with *Verbruggen's* untaught Airs, and her smiling repartees, the Audience were afraid they were going off the Stage [i.e., to bed] every Moment."

To get the repertory up and running took an enormous investment of energy, as breakaway companies periodically discovered. But once it was in place, it was fairly easy to keep going, so long as most of the actors worked conscientiously. The performance level for standard plays in a healthy company was probably fairly high. New plays were chancier, because they might not see more than three to six performances, total, and unless the actors were excited about a piece, their concentration could easily slip. In the same way, nowadays many symphony orchestras can play the standard repertory quite competently, and they know their specialties extremely well; but some resist the challenge of new work because of the extra demands it makes. Finding a balance is not easy.

To the twentieth-century reader, the plays of the period may not immediately seem attractive. They depict the top levels of a consciously hierarchical, male-dominated, urban society, one which was racist, sexist, and bigoted – and unashamed of any of these characteristics. The society portrayed in these plays had few ideals and few illusions.

Most of the characters in the comedies already have enough money not to work for a living; the rest are bent on gaining it. Their other concern is entertainment: sex, gossip, fashion. Having fun is serious business for them, because they don't have anything else to do. Money insulates them from the problems of their world as it insulates them from the weather, which in these plays is always fine. The range of their amusements is as limited as their social circles, and almost all of the fun is public and verbal, rather than private and physical. There are few lasting consequences to what the men do. Only fools gamble away their money, drink themselves into oblivion, or contact venereal diseases. Women's reputations may be threatened, but real consequences are seldom shown. There are no children in these comedies, even off-stage, just as there is no death in childbirth and no divorce that permitted remarriage. One might also question whether there is any love. One answer is that those who find love usually prepare to remove themselves from the game. The narrowness of concerns in these plays is easy to criticize, but the theatre played much the same part in social life that television sit-coms and soap operas play in the life of the United States at the end of the twentieth century. Is their selectivity so different from *As the World Turns*, *Dynasty*, and endless reruns of *M.A.S.H.*?

What of the original acting style? It is, of course, unrecapturable. Therefore, we must create our own interpretation of the scripts, without worrying too much about authenticity. Except that marriage is no longer the sole aim of all womankind, the power politics of relationships have not changed all that much. For those willing to take an unsentimental look at the ways some people interact, the plays can be bracing, and performers should not hesitate to experiment in animating the sometimes sketchy characters.

Judith Milhous is a Distinguished Professor at the Graduate Center of the City University of New York. She has written extensively about Restoration and 18th century theatre, including Thomas Betterton and the Management of Lincoln's Inn Fields, 1695-1708 *and (with Robert D. Hume)* Producible Interpretation: Eight English Plays, 1675-1707. *She has received several fellowships from the National Endowment for the Humanities, and has been the editor of* Theatre Survey *since 1990.*

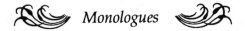 *Monologues*

This collection of monologues was performed as part of the 1992 Classics in Context Festival at Actors Theatre of Louisville. It is divided into three acts, each of which was originally designed to be played by six actors. However, a smaller or larger size cast can just as easily perform this collection of monologues, which can be further tailored to the performers by making substitutions from the additional monologues appended to the *Kiss and Tell* script.

THE WAY OF THE WORLD
by William Congreve

SPEAKER A:

> Of those few fools, who with ill stars are curs'd,
> Sure scribbling fools, call'd poets, fare the worst.
> For they're a sort of fools which fortune makes,
> And after she has made 'em fools, forsakes.

THE DOUBLE DEALER
by William Congreve

SPEAKER B:

> Moors, have this way (as story tells) to know
> Whether their brats are truly got, or no;
> Into the sea, the new-born babe is thrown,
> There, as instinct directs, to swim, or drown.
> A barbarous device, to try if spouse,
> Have kept religiously her nuptial vows!
>
> Such are the trials, poets make of plays:
> Only they trust to more inconstant seas;
> So, does our author, this his child commit
> To the tempestuous mercy of the pit,
> To know, if it be truly born of wit.

THE WONDER: A WOMAN KEEPS A SECRET
by Susanna Centlivre

SPEAKER C:

> Our author fears the critics of the stage,
> Who, like barbarians, spare no sex nor age;
> She trembles at those censors in the pit,
> Who think good-nature shews a want of wit.
> Such malice, Oh! What muse can undergo it?
> To save themselves, they always damn the poet.

THE DOUBLE DEALER
by William Congreve

SPEAKER D:

> Criticks avaunt; for you are fish of prey,
> And feed like sharks, upon an infant play.
> Be ev'ry monster of the deep away;
> Let's have a fair trial, and a clear sea.
>
> Let nature work, and do not damn too soon,
> For life will struggle long, 'ere it sink down:
> Let it at least rise thrice, before it drown.

THE MAN OF MODE
by George Etherege

SPEAKER E:

> For Heav'n be thanked, 'tis not so wise an age,
> But your own follies may supply the stage.
> 'Tis by your follies that we players thrive,
> As the physicians by diseases live.
> And as each year some new distemper reigns,

Whose friendly poison helps to increase their gains,
So among you, there starts up every day,
Some new unheard-of fool for us to play.
Then for your own sakes, be not too severe,
Nor what you all admire at home, damn here.
Since each is fond of his own ugly face,
Why should you, when we hold it, break the glass?

THE OLD BACHELOR
by William Congreve

PROLOGUE (FEMALE):
How this vile world is chang'd! In former days,
Prologues, were serious speeches, before plays;
Grave solemn things, as graces are to feasts;
Where, poets beg'd a blessing, from their guests.
But now, no more like suppliants, we come;
A play makes war, and prologue is the drum:
Arm'd with keen satyr, and with pointed wit,
We threaten you who do for judges sit,
To save our plays, or else we'll damn your pit.
But for your comfort, it falls out to day,
We've a young author and his first born play;
So, standing only on his good behaviour,
He's very civil, and entreats your favour.
Not but the man has malice, would he show it,
But on my conscience he's a bashful poet;
You think that strange—no matter, he'll out grow it.
Well, I'm his advocate—by me he prays you,
(I don't know whether I shall speak to please you)
He prays—O bless me! what shall I do now!
Hang me if I know what he prays, or how!
And 'twas the prettiest prologue, as he wrote it!
Well, the deuce take me, if I han't forgot it.
O Lord, for Heavens sake excuse the play,
Because, you know, if it be damn'd to day,

I shall be hang'd for wanting what to say,
For my sake then—but I'm in such confusion,
I cannot stay to hear your resolution.

THE ROVER; or THE BANISH'D CAVALIERS
by Aphra Behn

SPEAKER F:

As for the author of this coming play,
I ask'd him what he thought fit I should say,
In thanks for your good company to day:
He call'd me fool, and said it was well known,
You came not here for our sakes, but your own.

LOVE FOR LOVE
by William Congreve

Tattle, a foppish friend of the wealthy Foresight, plays his love game with the very naive Miss Prue, who is supposed to marry another. In his vainness, Tattle believes that every woman wants him and thus, his modus operandi is sound. In this instance, he succeeds. This is Tattle's and Miss Prue's first, but certainly not last, encounter.

TATTLE:

De'e you think you can love me? (*Miss Prue: Yes.*) Poo, pox, you must not say yes already. I shan't care a farthing for you then in a twinkling. Why you must say no, or you believe not, or you can't tell. Yes, if you would be well-bred. All well-bred persons lie. Besides, you are a woman, you must never speak what you think. Your words must contradict your thoughts, but your actions may contradict your words. So, when I ask you if you can love me, you must say no, but you must love me too. If I tell you you are handsome, you must deny it, and say I flatter you. But you must think yourself more charming than I speak you, and like me, for the beauty which I say you have, as much as if I had it myself. If I ask you to kiss me, you must be angry, but you must not refuse me. If I ask you for more, you must be more angry, but more complying. And as soon as ever I make you say you'll cry out, you must be sure to hold your tongue. Must I not lie too? Hum—yes. But you must believe I speak truth.

LOVE FOR LOVE
by William Congreve

Angelica, a young woman of considerable wealth and niece to the superstitious Foresight, decides to travel abroad when she learns that is where everyone in her circle is going. Her coach is broken, however, so she proceeds to manipulate her uncle into loaning her his.

ANGELICA:

Well, but I can neither make you a cuckold, uncle, by going abroad, nor secure you from being one by staying at home. But my inclinations are in force. I have a mind to go abroad, and if you won't lend me your coach, I'll take a hackney, or a chair, and leave you to erect a scheme, and find who's in conjunction with your wife. Why don't you keep her at home, if you're jealous when she's abroad? You know my aunt is a little retrograde (as you call it) in her nature. Uncle, I'm afraid you are not lord of the ascendant, ha, ha, ha. Nay, uncle, don't be angry. If you are, I'll reap up all your false prophecies, ridiculous dreams, and idle divinations. I'll swear you are a nuisance to the neighbourhood. What a bustle did you keep against the last invisible eclipse, laying in provision as 'twere for a siege! What a world of fire and candle, matches and tinderboxes did you purchase! One would have thought we were ever after to live underground, or at least making a voyage to Greenland, to inhabit there all the dark season. Nay, I'll declare how you prophesied popery was coming, only because the butler had mislaid some of the Apostle spoons, and thought they were lost. Away went religion and spoonmeat together. Indeed, uncle, I'll indite you for a wizard. Will you lend me your coach, or I'll go on.

LOVE FOR LOVE
by William Congreve

Ben, the sailor son of the wealthy Sir Sampson Legend, is brought back from his sea duties to marry the naive Miss Prue. However, he wants nothing to do with her and expresses his feelings to Mrs. Frail, a friend of the family, with whom he has pleaded his case previously.

BEN:

Why, father came and found me squabbling with yon chitty-faced thing, as he would have me marry, so he asked what was the matter. He asked in a surly sort of a way. It seems brother Val is gone mad, and so that put'n into a passion; but what, did I know that, what's that to me? So he asked in a surly sort of manner, and gad, I answered 'n as surlily. What tho he be my father, I an't bound prentice to 'n. So, faith I told 'n in plain terms, if I were minded to marry, I'd marry to please myself, not him. And for the young woman that he provided for me, I thought it more fitting for her to learn her sampler, and make dirt-pies, than to look after a husband. For my part I was none of her man. I had another voyage to make, let him take it as he will. Nay, nay, my mind run upon you, but I would not tell him so much. So he said he'd make my heart ache, and if so be that he could get a woman to his mind, he'd marry himself. Gad, says I, an you play the fool and marry at these years, there's no more danger of your head's aching than my heart. He was woundy angry when I gav'n that wipe. He hadn't a word to say, and so I left'n, and the green girl together. Mayhap the bee may bite, and he'll marry her himself, with all my heart. If I am undutiful and graceless, why did he beget me so? I did not get myself.

THE DOUBLE DEALER
by William Congreve

Lady Plyant, a woman caught in a marriage to a foolish old man, attempts to break up the engagement between her step-daughter Cynthia and Mellefont. After discussing her dissatisfaction with the engagement to her husband, she confronts Mellefont alone about his supposed passion for her.

LADY PLYANT:

Nay, nay, rise up, come you shall see my good nature. I know love is powerful, and no body can help his passion: 'Tis not your fault; nor I swear it is not mine,—how can I help it, if I have charms? And how can you help it, if you are made a captive? I swear it's pity it should be a fault,—but my honour—well, but your honour too—but the sin!—well but the necessity—O Lord, here's some body coming, I dare not stay. Well, you must consider of your crime; and strive as much as can be against it,— strive be sure—but don't be melancholy, don't despair,—but never think that I'll grant you any thing; O Lord, no,—but be sure you lay aside all thoughts of the marriage, for tho' I know you don't love Cynthia, only as a blind for your passion to me; yet it will make me jealous,—O Lord, what did I say? Jealous! no, no, I can't be jealous, for I must not love you,—therefore don't hope,—but don't despair neither,—O, they're coming, I must fly.

THE RELAPSE
by John VanBrugh

Loveless, married to Amanda, finds that he is drawn to Berinthia, his wife's cousin. He is puzzled by this attraction, as he still loves his wife. In a moment alone, he attempts to work out his dilemma.

LOVELESS:
Is my wife within?(*No.*)
'Tis well, leave me.
Sure, fate has yet some business to be done,
Before Amanda's heart and mine must rest;
Else, why amongst those legions of her sex,
Which throng the world,
Should she pick out for her companion
The only one on earth
Whom nature has endowed for her undoing?
Did she not rescue me, a groveling slave,
When chain'd and bound by that black tyrant vice,
I labour'd in its vilest drudgery?
Am I not strongly bound to love her for it?
To love her—Why, do I not love her then?
By earth and Heaven I do.
Nay, I have demonstration that I do:
For I would sacrifice my life to serve her.
Yet hold—if laying down my life
Be demonstration of my love,
What is't I feel in favour of Berinthia?
For should she be in danger, methinks, I could incline
To risk it for her service too; and yet I do not love her.
How then subsists my proof? –
– O, I have found it out.
What I would do for one, is demonstration of my love;
and if I'd do as much as for t'other, it there is demonstration of my friendship—Ay—it must be so. I find I'm very much her friend.—Yet let me ask myself one puzzling question more: Whence springs this mighty friendship all at once? For our acquaintance is of a later date. Now friendship's said to be a plant of tedious growth, its root composed of tender fibers, nice in their taste, cautious in spreading, checking with the least cor-

ruption in the soil, long ere it take, and longer still ere it appear to do so: whilst mine is in a moment shot so high, and fixed so fast, it seems beyond the power of storms to shake it. I doubt it thrives too fast. (*Enter Berinthia.*)

– Ah, she's here!—Nay, then, take heed, my heart, for there are dangers towards.

ACT II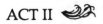

THE COUNTRY LASSES
by Charles Johnson

Excerpted from the prologue of an "innocent comedy," this piece differs from the libertine attitude of the Comedy of Manners. Rakes and country lasses engage in love and badinage, but conventional morality is upheld, not flouted, and the tale ends beneficently.

CHILD SPEAKER:

Make me to speak a prologue! Is he wild?
A prologue! Lord! are prologues for a child?
Such heathen words! So hard to bring 'em pat in!
The drama—Athens—God knows how much Latin!
But I must do't.
Plays, like ambassadors, in form are shewn,
When first they've public audience of the town;
The prologue ceremoniously harangues,
And moves your pity for the author's pangs;
Acquaints you that he stands behind the scenes,
And trembles for the fondling of his brains.
Our author seeks, like bards of—of—Oh! Greece,
To make his play and prologue of a piece;
He leads you to the rural scenes, to prove
The country bargain still is love for love.
Oh, Covent-Garden! nursery of ills!
Fam'd for consumption both of wit—and pills:
Who would not quit thy walks, and vice in fashion,
The doubts and fears of mercenary passion,
For safe complying nymphs, unknowing sinners,
A feast of unbought love in cleanly pinners!

Hold—what comes next? (*Looking on paper.*) I'll never say't, In short–
We've bigger actresses are fitter for't—
Lord, how you laugh! as 'twere some naughty joke.
Sure there's no wickedness in what I spoke.
How should I say such things, who never knew
What kissing meant, before I play'd Miss Prue?

THE WAY OF THE WORLD
by William Congreve

*Lady Wishfort asks her maid Foible to be her mirror and confidant
in anticipation of the arrival of her suitor Sir Rowland, who is
Waitwell in disguise. Waitwell is servant to Mirabell, an enemy of
Lady Wishfort. In yet another potentially humiliating prank,
Mirabell will have his man marry Foible and then court Lady
Wishfort.*

LADY WISHFORT:

And—well—and how do I look, Foible? Well, and how shall I
receive him? In what figure shall I give his heart the first impression? There is a great deal in the first impression. Shall I
sit?—No I won't sit—I'll walk—aye I'll walk from the door upon
his entrance; and then turn full upon him—No, that will be too
sudden. I'll lie—aye, I'll lie down—I'll receive him in my little
dressing room, there's a couch—Yes, yes, I'll give the first impression on a couch—I wont lie neither but loll and lean upon
one elbow; with one foot a little dangling off, jogging in a
thoughtful way—Yes—O, nothing is more alluring than a levee
from a couch in some confusion.—It shows the foot to advantage, and furnishes with blushes, and re-composing airs beyond
comparison. Hark! There's a coach.

THE MISTAKE
by John VanBrugh

Lopez enters the street alone, safe from the eyes and ears of his master Don Lorenzo. He waxes bravely about what he would say to his master who, having fallen in love with Leonora, has asked his servant to assist him in some nocturnal intrigue and wooing.

LOPEZ:

As soon as it is night, says my master to me, tho' it cost me my life, I'll enter Leonora's lodgings; therefore, make haste, Lopez, prepare every thing necessary. When my master said this to me, Sir, said I to my master (that is, I would have said it, if I had not been in such a fright I could say nothing; however, I'll say it to him now, and shall probably have a quiet hearing) "Look you, Sir, by dint of reason I intend to confound you. You are re-solved, you say, to get into Leonora's lodgings, tho' the devil stand in the doorway?—Yes, Lopez, that's my resolution—Very well; and what do you intend to do when you are there?—Why, what an injured man should do, make her sensible of—Make her sensible of a pudding! Don't you see she's a jade? She'll raise the house about your ears, arm the whole family, set the great dog at you—Were there three legions of devils to repulse me, in such a cause I could disperse them all—Why, then you have no occasion for help, Sir; you may leave me at home to lay the cloth—No, thou art my ancient friend, my fellow-traveller; and to reward thy faithful services, this night thou shalt partake my danger and my glory—Sir, I have got glory enough under you already to content any reasonable servant for his life—Thy mod-esty makes me willing to double my bounty; this night may bring eternal honour to thee and thy family—Eternal honor, sir, is too much in conscience for a serving-man; besides, ambition has been many a great soul's undoing—I doubt thou art afraid, my Lopez; thou shalt be armed with back, with breast, and head-piece—They will incumber me in my retreat—Retreat, my hero! thou never shalt retreat—Then, by my troth, I'll never go, Sir.' But here he comes.

THE DOUBLE DEALER
by William Congreve

Maskwell has persuaded Melefont that the former's plot with Cynthia's jealous aunt to break the match between Cynthia and Mellefont is actually in the service of securing the marriage between those promised lovers. True to his character, Maskwell tells the audience his intrigues, which he believes are so well concealed he can share them with impunity with his victims.

MASKWELL:

Ha! but is there not such a thing as honesty? Yes, and whosoever has it about him, bears an enemy in his breast: For your honest man, as I take it, is that nice, scrupulous, conscientious person, who will cheat no body but himself ; such another coxcomb, as your wise man, who is too hard for all the world, and will be made a fool of by no body, but himself: Ha, ha, ha. Well for wisdom and honesty, give me cunning and hypocrisie; oh 'tis such a pleasure, to angle for fair-faced fools! then that hungry gudgeon credulity, will bite at any thing—Why, let me see, I have the same face, the same words and accents, when I speak what I do think; and when I speak what I do not think—the very same—and dear dissimulation is the only art, not to be known from nature.

Why will mankind be fools, and be deceiv'd?
And why are friends and lovers oaths believ'd;
When each, who searches strictly his own mind,
May so much fraud and power of baseness find?

THE ROVER; OR THE BANISH'D CAVALIERS
by Aphra Behn

Angellica Bianca, a famous courtesan, experiences love for the first time by falling for the philandering cavalier Willmore. In this scene, brandishing a pistol which she holds to his breast, she expresses her anger and sense of betrayal after having found him paying court to another woman.

ANGELLICA:

>You said you loved me.
>And at that instant I gave you my heart.
>I'd pride enough and love enough to think
>That it could raise thy soul above the vulgar,
>Nay, make you all soul too, and soft and constant.
>Why did you lie and cheapen me? Alas,
>I thought all men were born to be my slaves,
>And wore my power like lightning in my eyes;
>But when love held the mirror, that cruel glass
>Reflected all the weakness of my soul;
>My pride was turned to a submissive passion
>And so I bowed, which I ne'er did before
>To anyone or anything but heaven.
>I thought that I had won you and that you
>Would value me the higher for my folly.
>But now I see you gave me no more than dog lust,
>Made me your spaniel bitch; and so I fell
>Like a long-worshipped idol at the last
>Perceived a fraud, a cheat, a bauble. Why
>Didst thou destroy my too long fancied power?
>Why didst thou give me oaths? Why didst thou kneel
>And make me soft? Why, why didst thou enslave me?
>Ah, sir, ah, sir, I yet had been content
>To wear my chains with vanity and joy,
>Hadst thou not broke those vows that put them on.

OROONOKO
by Thomas Southerne

The once powerful but now captured leader of the West African nation of Angola finds himself overwhelmed more by grief than captivity. Blanford, one of the captors, has won Oroonoko's trust and becomes the willing listener to the great warrior's story of his beloved. This heroic tragedy was adapted from a novel by Aphra Behn.

OROONOKO:
> Let me talk whole days
> Of my Imoinda. O! I'll tell thee all
> From first to last; and pray observe me well.
> There was a stranger in my father's court,
> Valu'd and honour'd much: He was a white,
> The first I ever saw of your complexion:
> He chang'd his gods for ours, and so grew great;
> Of many virtues, and so fam'd in arms,
> He still commanded all my father's wars.
> I was bred under him. One fatal day,
> The armies joining, he before me stept,
> Receiving in his breast a poison'd dart
> Levell'd at me; he dy'd within my arms.
> He left an only daughter, whom he brought
> An infant to Angola. When I came
> Back to the court, a happy conqueror;
> Humanity oblig'd me to condole
> With this sad virgin for a father's loss,
> Lost for my safety. I presented her
> With all the slaves of battle to attone
> Her father's ghost. But when I saw her face
> And heard her speak, I offer'd up my self
> To be the sacrifice. She bow'd and blush'd;
> I wonder'd and ador'd. The sacred pow'r
> That had subdu'd me, then inspir'd my tongue,
> Inclin'd her heart; and all our talk was Love.
> O! I was too happy.
> I marry'd her: And though my country's custom
> Indulg'd the privilege of many wives,

I swore my self never to know but her.
She grew with child, and I grew happier still.
O my Imoinda! but it cou'd not last.
Her fatal beauty reach'd my father's ears:
He sent for her to court, where, cursed court!
No woman comes, but for his amorous use.
He raging to possess her, she was forc'd
To own her self my wife. The furious King
Started at incest: But grown desperate,
Not daring to enjoy what he desir'd,
In mad revenge, which I cou'd never learn,
He poison'd her, or sent her far, far off,
Far from my hopes ever to see her more.
I have done.
I'll trouble you no farther: now and then,
A sigh will have its way; that shall be all.

ACT III 🌶

THE RELAPSE
by John VanBrugh

*The quintessential fop, Lord Foppington expounds indigently
upon his daily habits before uninterested company.*

LORD FOPPINGTON:
To my mind the inside of a book, is to entertain one's self with
the forced product of another man's brain. Now, I think, a man
of quality and breeding, may be much diverted with the natural
sprouts of his own. Once he comes to know this town, he finds
so many better ways of passing away the four and twenty
hours, that 'twere ten thousand pities he should consume his
time in reading. For example, Madam, my life; my life, Madam,
is a perpetual stream of pleasure, that glides through with such
a variety of entertainments, I believe the wisest of our ancestors
never had the least conception; not that I pretend to be a beau;
but a man must endeavour to look wholesome, lest he makes so
nauseous a figure in the side-box, the ladies should be com-
pelled to turn their eyes upon the play. So at ten o'clock, I say, I
rise. Now, if I find it a good day, I resolve to take a turn in the
park, and see the fine women; so huddle on my clothes, and get
dressed by one. If it be nasty weather, I take a turn in the chocolate house; where, as you walk, Madam, you have the prettiest
prospect in the world: you have looking glasses all around
you—But I'm afraid I tire the company. Not at all? Why then,
ladies, from thence I go to dinner at Lacket's, and there you are
so nicely and delicately served, that, stop my vitals, they can
compose you a dish, no bigger than a saucer, shall come to fifty
shillings; between eating my dinner, and washing my mouth,
ladies, I spend my time, till I go to the play; where till nine
o'clock, I entertain myself with looking upon the company; and

usually dispose of one hour more in leading them out. So there's twelve of the four and twenty pretty well over. The other twelve, Madam, are disposed of in two articles: in the first four I toast myself drunk, and in t'other eight I sleep myself sober again. Thus, ladies, you see my life is an eternal round O of delights.

THE PROVOK'D WIFE
by John VanBrugh

After being abused yet again by her boorish, indolent husband, the unhappily married Lady Brute weighs faithfulness against happiness.

LADY BRUTE:

The devil's in the fellow, I think—I was told before I married him, that thus 'twou'd be: But I thought I had charms enough to govern him; and that where there was an estate, a woman must needs be happy; so my vanity has deceiv'd me, and my ambition has made me uneasy. But there's some comfort still; if one wou'd be reveng'd of him, these are good times; a woman may have a gallant, and a separate maintenance too—I never lov'd him, yet I have been ever true to him; and that, in spite of all the attacks of art and nature upon a poor weak woman's heart, in favour of a tempting lover. Methinks so noble a defence as I have made, shou'd be rewarded with a better usage—Or who can tell?—Perhaps a good part of what I suffer from my husband, may be a judgment upon me for my cruelty to my lover.—Lord, with what pleasure could I indulge that thought, were there but a possibility of finding arguments to make it good!—And how do I know but there may?—Let me see—What opposes?—My matrimonial vow—Why, what did I vow? I think I promis'd to be true to my husband. Well; and he promis'd to be kind to me. But he han't kept his word—Why then I'm absolv'd from mine—Ay, that seems clear to me. The argument's good between the king and the people, why not between the husband and the wife? Well, by all I see, if I argue the matter a little longer with myself, I shan't find so many bugbears in the way as I thought I shou'd. Lord, what fine notions of virtue do we women take up upon the credit of old foolish philosophers! Virtue's its own reward, virtue's this, virtue's that—Virtue's an ass, and a gallant's worth forty on't.

THE DRUMMER
by Joseph Addison

Recently widowed after a happy marriage, Lady Truman justifies her attentions toward one of her many suitors.

LADY TRUMAN:

Women who have been happy in a first marriage, are the most apt to venture upon a second. But, for my part, I had a husband so every way suited to my inclinations, that I must entirely forget him, before I can like another man. I have now been a widow but fourteen months, and have had twice as many lovers, all of them professed admirers of my person, but passionately in love with my jointure. I think it is a revenge I owe my sex, to make an example of this worthless tribe of fellows, who grow impudent, dress themselves fine, and fancy we are obliged to provide for them. But of all my captives, Mr. Tinsel is the most extraordinary in his kind. I hope the diversion I give myself with him is unblameable. I'm sure 'tis necessary to turn my thoughts off from the memory of that dear man, who has been the greatest happiness and affliction of my life. My heart would be a prey to melancholy, if I did not find these innocent methods of relieving it. Now, Mr. Tinsel, there's a wild fellow. 'Tis a thousand pities he should be lost; I should be mighty glad to reform him.

THE WAY OF THE WORLD
by William Congreve

Millimant, a well bred, intelligent young lady with many admirers, is in love with her suitor Mirabell. In response to Mirabell's proposal of marriage, Millimant sets forth her conditions for making the marriage tolerable.

MILLIMANT:
My dear liberty, shall I leave thee? My faithful solitude, my darling contemplation, must I bid you then adieu? ay-h adieu—my morning thoughts, agreeable wakings, indolent slumbers, all ye *doucers, ye Someils du Matin*, adieu—I can't do't, 'tis more than impossible—positively Mirabell, I'll lie a bed in a morning as long as I please, and dee hear, I won't be call'd names after I'm married, positively I won't be call'd names. Ay as wife, spouse, my dear, joy, jewel, love, sweetheart and the rest of that nauseous cant, in which men and their wives are so fulsomely familiar,—I shall never bear that,—Good Mirabell don't let us be familiar or fond, nor kiss before folks, like my Lady Fadler and Sir Francis: Nor goe to Hide Park together the first Sunday in a new chariot, to provoke eyes and whispers; And then never to be seen there together again; as if we were proud of one another the first week, and asham'd of one another for ever after. Let us never visit together nor go to a play together, But let us be very strange and well bred: let us be as strange as if we had been married a great while; and as well bred as if we were not marri'd at all. Also liberty to pay and receive visits to and from whom I please, to write and receive letters, without Interrogatories or wry faces on your part. To wear what I please; and choose conversation with regard only to my own taste; to have no obligation upon me to converse with wits that I don't like, because they are your acquaintance; or to be intimate with fools, because they may be your relations. Come to dinner when I please, dine in my dressing room when I'm out of humour without giving a reason. To have my closet inviolate; to be sole Empress of my tea-table, which you must never presume to approach without first asking leave. And lastly, wherever I am, you shall always knock at the door before you come in. These articles subscrib'd, If I continue to endure you a little longer, I may by degrees dwindle into a wife.

THE WAY OF THE WORLD
by William Congreve

*Lady Millimant's suitor and intellectual equal, Mirabell responds
to Millimant's exacting conditions of the marriage proposal with
his own compromises and provisos.*

MIRABELL:

Imprimis then, I covenant that your acquaintance be general;
that you admit no sworn confident, or intimate of your own sex;
No she friend to screen her affairs under your countenance and
tempt you to make trial of a mutual secresie. No decoy-duck to
wheadle you a fop—scrambling to the play in a mask—then
bring you home in a pretended fright, when you think you shall
be found out. Item, I article, that you continue to like your own
face, as long as I shall. And while it passes current with me, that
you endeavour not to new coin it. To which end, together with
all vizards for the day, I prohibit all masks for the night, made of
oil'd skins and I know not what—hog's-bones, hare's-gall, pig-
water, and the marrow of a roasted cat. In short, I forbid all
commerce with the gentlewoman in what-de-call-it-court. Item,
I shut my doors against all bauds with baskets, and penny-
worths of muslin, china, fans, atlases, &c.—Item, when you shall
be breeding—which may be presum'd, with a blessing on our
endeavours—I denounce against all strait-lacing, squeezing for
a shape, till you mold my boy's head like a sugar-loaf; and instead of a man-child, make me the father to a crooked-billet.
Lastly to the dominion of the tea-table, I submit.—But with proviso, that you exceed not in your province; but restrain your self
to native and simple tea-table drinks, as tea, chocolate and coffee. As likewise to genuine and, authoriz'd tea-table talk,—such
as mending of fashions, spoiling reputations, railing at absent
friends, and so forth—but that on no account you encroach
upon the mens prerogative, and presume to drink healths, or
toast fellows; for prevention of which; I banish all foreign forces,
all auxiliaries to the tea-table, as orange-brandy, all anniseed,
cinnamon, citron and barbado's-waters, together with ratifia
and the most noble spirit of clary,—but for cowslip-wine,
poppy-water and all dormitives, those I allow,—these proviso's
admitted, in other things I may prove a tractable and complying

husband. Then we're agreed. Shall I kiss your hand upon the contract?

SIR HARRY WILDAIR
by George Farquhar

*After sitting through an English play, an enraged Frenchman
rails against the manners and customs of his enemy the English,
and threatens to ruin the play.*

FRIEND:
Ventre bleu! vere is dis dam poet? vere
Garcon! me vil cut off all his two ear:
Je suis enragé—now he is not here.
He has affront de French! Le vilaine bête!
De French! your best friend!—you suffre dat?
Parbleu! Messieurs, il serait fort ingrate!
Vat have you English, dat you can call your own!
Vat have you of grand pleasure in dis town,
Vidout it come from France, dat vil go down?
Picquet, basset; your vin, your dress, your dance;
'Tis all, you see, tout a-la-mode de France.
De beau dere buy a hondre knick-knack;
He carry out wit, but seldome bring it back:
But den he bring a snuff-box hinge, so small
De joint, you can no see de vark at all,
Cost him five pistoles, dat is sheap enough,
In tree year it sal save half and ounce of snoffe.
De coquet, she ave her ratifia dere,
Her gown, her complexion, deux yeux, her lovere.
As for de cuckold—dat indeed you can make here.
De French it is dat teach the lady wear
De short muff, wit her vite elbow bare;
De beau de large muff, wit his sleeve down dere.
Ve teach your vifes to ope dere husband's purses,
To put de Furbelo round dere coach, and dere horses.
Garçon! ve teach you every ting de varle;
For vy den your damn poet dare to snarle?
Begar, me vil be revenge upon his play,
Tree tousan refugee (parbleu c'est vrai)
Sall all come here, and damn him upon his tird day.

EPILOGUES

SHE WOULD AND SHE WOULD NOT
by Colley Cibber

SPEAKER A:

'Mongst all the rules the ancients had in vogue,
We find no mention of an epilogue,
Which plainly shows they're innovations, brought
Since rules, design, and nature, were forgot;
The custom therefore our next play shall break,
But now a joyful motive bids us speak.

THE DOUBLE DEALER
by William Congreve

SPEAKER B:

Could poets but forsee how plays would take,
Then they could tell what epilogues to make;
Whether to thank, or blame their audience, most:
But that late knowledge, does much hazard cost,
Till dice are thrown, there's nothing won, nor lost.

SPEAKER C:

All have a right and title to some part,
Each choosing that, in which he has most art.
The dreadful men of learning, all confound,
Unless the fable's good, and moral sound.
The vizor-masks, that are in pit and gallery,
Approve, or damn the repartee and rallery.

SPEAKER D:

The lady criticks, who are better read,
Enquire if characters are nicely bred;

If the soft things are penn'd and spoke with grace;
They judge of action too, and time, and place;
In which, we do not doubt but they're discerning,
For that's a kind of assignation learning.

THE WAY OF THE WORLD
by William Congreve

SPEAKER E:
    After our epilogue this crowd dismisses,
    I'm thinking how this play'll be pull'd to pieces.
    But pray consider, ere you doom its fall,
    How hard a thing 'twould be, to please you all.
SPEAKER F:
    There are some criticks so with spleen diseas'd,
    They scarcely come inclining to be pleas'd:
    And sure he must have more than mortal skill,
    Who pleases any one against his will.

Kiss and Tell
Additional Monologues—for Women

THE BEAUX' STRATEGEM
by George Farquhar

*Mrs. Sullen was married off by her parents to a rather crude and
vulgar man, Sullen, and therefore had to move from London to
live with him and Mrs. Bountiful at their country estate. Here
Mrs. Sullen bemoans the misery of sharing her husband's bed.*

MRS. SULLEN:
O sister, sister! if you ever marry, beware of a sullen, silent sot,
one that's always musing but never thinks. There's some diversion in a talking blockhead; and since a woman must wear
chains, I would have the pleasure of hearing 'em rattle a little.
Now you shall see, but take this by the way. He came home this
morning at his usual hour of four, wakened me out of a sweet
dream of something else, by tumbling over the tea-table, which
he broke all to pieces; after his man and he had rolled about the
room, like sick passengers in a storm, he comes flounce into bed,
dead as a salmon into a fishmonger's basket; his feet as cold as
ice, his breath hot as a furnace, and his hands and his face as
greasy as his flannel night-cap. O matrimony! He tosses up the
clothes with a barbarous swing over his shoulders, disorders the
whole economy of my bed, leaves me half naked and my whole
night's comfort is the tuneable serenade of that wakeful nightin-
gale, his nose! Oh, the pleasure of counting the melancholy clock
by a snoring husband!

LOVES'S LAST SHIFT
by Colley Cibber

The virtuous Amanda poses as a seductive mistress in order to trick her newly returned husband Loveless, who had abandoned her ten years before, into rediscovering his passion for her. The next morning she confronts him with his cruelty.

AMANDA:

I'll give you ease immediately.—Since then you have allowed a woman may be virtuous—how will you excuse the man who leaves the bosom of a wife so qualified, for the abandoned pleasures of a deceitful prostitute; ruins her fortune, contemns her counsel, loaths her bed, and leaves her to the lingering miseries of despair and love? while, in return of all these wrongs, she, his poor forsaken wife, meditates no revenge, but what her piercing tears, and secret vows to heaven for his conversion yields her; yet still loves on, is constant and unshaken to the last. Can you believe that such a man can live without the stings of conscience, "and yet be master of his senses?" Conscience? Did you ne'er feel the checks of it? Did it never, never tell you of your broken vows?

THE ROVER; OR THE BANISH'D CAVALIERS
by Aphra Behn

ANGELLICA:

I would not stay one month longer in this town, Moretta, but for the vanity and pleasure to see and be seen. While the old general lived, his jealousy kept me dead to the world, neither seen nor enjoyed. I had been still as chaste as a nunnery prayer, had my mind been as innocent as his bed. I'll seek my pleasure now and leave a name and memory behind me. The novelty and humour of this device will breed discourse. I know there's few are like to give the money; nor want I any neither. Yet I'll have the gusto to see them gaze and sigh and wish for what they may not purchase. And when our nine days' wonder's over, we'll be gone. Nay, I would eat bran ere any he in breeches in this place should come between my sheets. Here's Don Pedro again an another too. I'll fetch my lute, for 'tis for one of these that I have spread my nets.

THE COUNTRY WIFE
by William Wycherly

Naive but nonetheless clever, Mrs. Pinchwife substitutes a letter delaring her passion for her newfound love Mr. Horner for the vicious "Dear John" letter her jealous husband had forced her to write.

MRS. PINCHWIFE:

"For Mr Horner"—So, I am glad he has told me his name. Dear Mr Horner! But why should I send thee such a letter that will vex thee, and make thee angry with me?—Well, I will not send it. —Ay, but then my husband will kill me, for I see plainly he won't let me love Mr Horner—but what care I for my husband?—I won't, so I won't, send poor Mr Horner such a letter—but then my husband—But oh—what if I writ at bottom my husband made me write it?—Ay, but then my husband would see't. —Can one have no shift? Ah, a London woman would have had a hundred presently. Stay—what if I should write a letter, and wrap it up like this, and write on't too? Ay, but then my husband would see't.—I don't know what to do.—But yet y'vads, I'll try, so I will—for I will not send this letter to poor Mr Horner, come what will on't. (*She writes, and repeats what she hath writ.*) "Dear, sweet Mr Horner"—so-"my husband would have me send you a base, rude, unmannerly letter—but I won't"—so—"and would have me say to you that I hate you, poor Mr Horner—but I won't tell a lie for him"—there—"for I'm sure if you and I were in the country at cards together"—so—"I could not help treading on your toe under the table"—so—"or rubbing knees with you, and staring in your face till you saw me"—very well—"and then looking down, and blushing for an hour together"—so—"but I must make haste before my husband come; and now he has taught me to write letters, you shall have longer ones from me, who am Dear, dear, poor dear Mr Horner,
your most humble friend,
and servant to command 'till death,
Margery Pinchwife."

THE WONDER: A WOMAN KEEPS A SECRET
by Susanna Centlivre

*Unable to persuade her father to free her from an unwanted match,
Isabella jumps from her window in desperation. Fortuitously, she
is caught by Colonel Briton, who, through a string of coincidences,
delivers the faint Isabella to the home of Donna Violante, her ex-
iled brother's mistress. There she relates her story.*

ISABELLA:

Ha! where am I? What kind star preserved and lodged me here?
Oh! I remember now. Forgive me, dear Violante! My thought
ran so much upon the danger I escap'd I forgot. (*Violante: May I
not know your story?*) I have often told thee that my father design'd to sacrifice me to Don Guzman, who, it seems, is just return'd from Holland, and expected ashore to—morrow, the day
that he has set to celebrate our nuptials. Upon my refusing to
obey him, he lock'd me into my chamber, vowing to keep me
there till he arriv'd, and force me to consent. I know my father to
be positive, never to be won from his design; and having no
hope left me to escape the marriage, I leap'd from the window
into the street. A gentleman passing by by accident, caught me
up in his arms: at first, my fright made me apprehend it was my
father, till he assured me to the contrary. I desired the stranger
to convey me to the next monastery, but ere I reach'd the door, I
saw, or fanc'd I saw, Lissardo, my brother's man, and the
thought that his master might not be far off flung me into a
swoon, which is all I can remember.

THE WONDER: A WOMAN KEEPS A SECRET
by Susanna Centlivre

Isabella's tyrannical father, Don Lopez, has arranged a marriage between his daughter and Don Guzman, an old and foolish—but rich—man. Isabella, in conversation with her maid Inis, resolves to become a nun rather than bow to the unjust customs of her country, which dictate she must obey her father.

ISABELLA:

The thoughts of a husband is as terrible to me as the sight of a hobgoblin. To be forced into the arms of an idiot, "a sneaking, snivelling, drivelling, avaricious fool!" who has neither person to please the eye, sense to charm the ear, nor generosity to supply those defects. Ah, Inis! What pleasant lives women lead in England, where duty wears not fetter but inclination! The custom of our country enslaves us from our very cradles, first to our parents, next to our husbands, and when Heaven is so kind to rid us of both these, our brothers still usurp authority, and expect a blind obedience from us; so that maids, wives or widows, we are little better than slaves to the tyrant, man. Therefore, to avoid their power, I resolve to cast myself into a monastery. There will be no man to plague me.

THE WONDER: A WOMAN KEEPS A SECRET
by Susanna Centlivre

This epilogue was spoken by the actress playing Donna Isabella. It follows a happy ending, in which the romantic lead, Don Felix, declares women his equal: "That man has no advantage, but the name."

EPILOGUE:
Custom, with all our modern laws combin'd,
Has given such power despotic to mankind,
That we have only so much virtue now
As they are pleas'd in favour to allow;
Thus, like mechanic work, we're us'd with scorn,
And wound up only for a present turn.
Some are for having our whole sex enslav'd,
Affirming we'ave no souls, and cann't be sav'd;
But were the women all of my opinion,
We'd soon shake off this false, usurp'd dominion,
We'd make the tyrants own that we cou'd prove
As fit for other bus'ness as for love.
Lord! what prerogative might we obtain,
Could we from yielding a few months refrain!
How fondly would our dangling lovers date!
What homage wou'd be paid to petticoat!
'Twou'd be a jest to see the change of fate;
How might we all of politics debate,
Promise and swear what we ne'er meant to do,
And, what's harder, keep our secrets too.

THE COUNTRY LASSES
by Charles Johnson

Epilogue to the play, spoken by Aura dressed in boy's clothes.

AURA:
 Critics, the poet's champion here I stand;
 Lo! in his name, the combat I demand;
 'Tis my opinion that his cause is good,
 And I'll defend it with my heart's best blood;
 I'll push you, my bold boys, the round parade
 Cart over arm, or terse, or flanconnade.
 —Codso! these breeches have so fired my brain,
 I shan't be easy till I've kill'd my man:
 What! not one beau step forth to give me battle;
 Where are those pretty things that used to tattle
 Such tender nonsense?—But they're all so civil
 They hate a naked weapon; 'tis the devil.
 —Now let me die, my dear, Sir Coxcomb cries,
 You want no other weapons, but your eyes.
 I hate these fawning triflers, and declare
 Against all smock-faced critics open war.
 Know, gentlemen, the poet's my ally,
 And I'll defend him to the last, or die;
 My sword is out; I'll never basely sue,
 Nor sheath it while my enemy's in view;
 No bribes, no tricks, no wheedling of my face,
 Include us both i'th' treaty, if you please;
 But faith, I'll never make a separate peace.
 No, ye French heroes, I'll not take your word,
 You'll beat a man when you have got his sword;
 Ay, that's your play—I know ye, Sirs, of old,
 You bully like the devil—with your gold;
 What must we do, then?—Settle plenipo's,
 And bravely, sword in hand, treat with our foes.
 To you we fly, ye charitable fair,
 To put an end to this dramatic war;
 Your smiles will cause all hostile acts to cease,
 And make a lasting, honourable peace.

THE REFUSAL
by Colley Cibber

Sophrenia has offered to assist her mother in forcing an undesirable marriage onto her younger sister, Charlotte, because the sisters are vying for the same gentleman. Deemed the wiser sister, Sophrenia's attempt to rise above issues of gender come into conflict with her own romantic passions. Hence, this critical appraisal of her mother proves highly ironic.

SOPHRENIA:

Yes, I shall assist you, Madam; though not to gratify your resentments, but my own. Poor lady! Is this then all the fruit of your philosophy? Is this her conduct of the passions, not to endure another should possess what she pretends to scorn? Are these her self-denials? Where, where was her self-examination all this while? The least inquiry there had shown these passions as they are: then had she seen, that all this anger at my sister was but envy: those reproaches on her lover, jealousy: even that jealousy, the child of vanity, and her avowed resentment, malice! Good Heaven! Can she be this creature, and know it not?—And yet 'tis so—so partial's Nature to herself,

That charity begins, where knowledge should,
And all our wisdom's counsell'd by the blood:
The faults of others we with ease discern,
But our own frailties are the last we learn.

LOVE'S LAST SHIFT
by Colley Cibber

The virtuous Amanda poses as a seductive mistress in order to trick her wandering husband into returning to her. As she prepares to reveal her identity, she wonders if her scheme will be successful.

AMANDA:

Thus far my hopes have all been answered, and my disguise of vicious love has charm'd him ev'n to a madness of impure desire.—but now I tremble to pull off the mask, lest barefac'd virtue should fright him from my arms forever. Yet sure there are charms in virtue, nay, stronger and more pleasing far than hateful vice can boast of; else why have holy martyrs perished for its sake? while lewdness ever gives severe repentance and unwilling death.—Good heaven inspire my heart, and hang upon my tongue the force of truth and eloquence, that I may lure this wandering falcon back to love and virtue.—He comes, and now my dreadful talk begins.

Kiss and Tell
Additional Monologues—for Men

THE CONSTANT COUPLE
by George Farquhar

*Sir Harry Wildair, an "airy Gentleman affecting humorous
Gaiety and Freedom in his Behaviour," is never out of sorts. When
Lady Lurewell tell the good-natured Sir Harry that Smuggler, the
town Alderman, has accused him of dishonorable dealings, Sir
Harry laughingly picks up a cudgel and "in jest" beats the old
man soundly. He then relates his satisfaction with the deed.*

SIR HARRY WILDAIR:
   How pleasant is resenting an injury without passion!
   'Tis the beauty of revenge.
   Let statesmen plot, and under business groan,
   And settling public quiet, lose their own;
   Let soldiers drudge and fight for pay or fame,
   For when they're shot, I think 'tis much the same;
   Let scholars vex their brains with mood and tense,
   And, mad with strength of reason, fools commence,
   Losing their wits in searching after sense;
   Their summum bonum they must toil to gain,
   And seeking pleasure, spend their life in pain.
   I make the most of life, no hour mis-spend.
   Pleasure's the mean, and pleasure is my end.
   No spleen, no trouble shall my time destroy;
   Life's but a span, I'll every inch enjoy.

THE REHEARSAL
by George Villiers, 2nd Duke of Buckingham

Prince Volscius, a character in "modern" playwright Bayes' non-sensical play-within-a-play, is forced to choose between love and honor. To the dismay and amazement of his critics, the insufferable Bayes has embodied the Prince's struggle in his footwear. The young royal debates his fate—boots on, or boots off?

PRINCE VOLSCIUS:
> My legs, the emblem of my various thought,
> Shew to what sad distraction I am brought:
> Sometimes with stubborn honor, like this boot,
> My mind is guarded, and resolved to do't :
> Sometimes again, that very mind, by love
> Disarmed, like this other leg does prove.
> Shall I to honor, or to love give way?
> Go on, cries honor; tender love says, nay:
> Honor aloud commands, pluck both boots on;
> But softer love does whisper, put on none.
> What shall I do? What conduct shall I find,
> To lead me through this twilight of my mind?
> For as a bright day, with black approach of night,
> Contending, makes a doubtful puzzling light;
> So does my honor, and my love together,
> Puzzle me so, I can resolve for neither.

THE DOUBLE DEALER
by William Congreve

Maskwell, the "Double Dealer," betrays his friend Mellefont: he invites Lord Touchwood to witness a scene in which it appears that Mellefont is trying to seduce Lady Touchwood. Aware that his motives for hurting his friend will be questioned, Maskwell purposefully lets Lord Touchwood overhear him talking of his "secret" love for Cynthia, Mellefont's betrothed.

MASKWELL:

What have I done? 'Twas honest—And shall I be rewarded for it? No, 'twas honest, therefore I shan't;—Nay, rather, therefore I ought not; for it rewards itself. But it should be known! then I have lost a friend! He was an ill man, and I have gain'd; for half I have served myself, and what is yet better, I have served a worthy Lord to whom I owe myself. Yet, I am wretched—O there is a secret burns within this breast, which should it once blaze forth, would ruine all, consume my honest character, and brand me with the name of villain. Why do I love ! yet Heaven and my waking conscience are my witnesses, I never gave one working thought a vent; which might discover that I lov'd, nor ever must; no, let it prey upon my heart; for I would rather die, than seem once, barely dishonest:—O, should it be known I love fair Cynthia , all this that I have done, would look like rivals malice, false friendship to my lord, and base self-interest. Let me perish first, and from this hour avoid all sight and speech, and, if I can, all thought of that pernicious beauty. Ha! but what is my distraction doing? I am wildly talking to myself, and some ill chance might have directed malicious ears this way.

LOVE FOR LOVE
by William Congreve

Mr. Tattle defends his reputation as a "keeper of ladies' secrets" to a skeptical crowd, even as he "accidentally" lets details of his past liaisons slip.

TATTLE:

Well, my witnesses are not present, but I confess I have had favours from persons. But as the favours are numberless, so the persons are nameless. I can shew letters, lockets, pictures and rings; and if there be occasion for witnesses, I can summon the maids at the chocolate houses, all the porters of Pall-Mall and Covent-Garden, the door-keepers at the Playhouse, the drawers at Locket's, Pontack's, the Rummer, Spring-Garden; my own landlady and valet de chambre, all who shall make oath that I receive more letters than the secretary's office, and that I have more vizor-masks to enquire for me than ever went to see the hermaphrodite or the naked prince. And it is notorious that in a country church once, an enquiry being made who I was, it was answered I was the famour Tattle, who had ruined so many women. True: I was called Turk Tattle all over the parish. The next Sunday all the old women kept their daughters at home, and the parson had not half his congregation. He would have brought me into the Spiritual Court, but I was revenged upon him, for he had a handsome daughter whom I initiated into the science. But I repented it afterwards, for it was talked of in town. And a lady of quality that shall be nameless, in a raging fit of jealousy, came down in her coach and six horses and exposed herself upon my account. Gad, I was sorry for it with all my heart—you know whom I mean. You know where we raffled—Gadso, the heat of my story carried me beyond my discretion, as the heat of the lady's passion hurried her beyond her reputation. But I hope you don't know on whom I mean; for there were a great many ladies raffled. Pox on't, now could I bite off my tongue.

THE ROVER; OR THE BANISH'D CAVALIERS
by Aphra Behn

BLUNT:

A pox on this tailor, for not yet bringing home the clothes I bespoke! And a pox of all poor cavaliers! A man can never keep a spare suit for 'em, and I shall have these rogues come in and find me naked. There's the worst of all—the colonel and Willmore, that rogue, will abuse me out of all Christian patience. But I'm resolved to arm myself: the rascals shall not insult over me too much. What a dog was I to believe woman, to be thus soothed into a cozening. (Puts on an old rusty sword and buff belt.) A fine ladylike whore to cheat me thus. A pox light on her, I shall never be reconciled to the sex more. What would I give her to have one of 'em within my reach now! Any mortal thing in petticoats, on whom to be revenged. But, here's a cursed book,—that can instruct me how to prevent such mischiefs now 'tis too late. Well, 'tis a rare convenient thing to read a little now and then to ease the mind. O dog. O silly dog!

THE COUNTRY WIFE
by William Wycherly

The violently jealous Mr. Pinchwife discovers his young wife writing a letter to her lover, the womanizing Mr. Horner, and threatens her life.

PINCHWIFE:

How's this? nay, you shall not stir, madam:—"Dear, dear, dear Mr. Horner"—very well—I have taught you to write letters to good purpose—but let us see't. "First, I am to beg your pardon for my boldness in writing to you, which I'd have you to know I would not have done, had not you said first you loved me so extremely, which if you do, you will suffer me to lie in the arms of another man whom I loathe, nauseate, and detest."—Now you can write these filthy words. But what follows?—"Therefore, I hope you will speedily find some way to free me from this unfortunate match, which was never, I assure you, of my choice, but I'm afraid 'tis already too far gone; however, if you love me, as I do you, you will try what you can do; but you must help me away before tomorrow, or else, alas! I shall be forever out of your reach, for I can defer no longer our—our—" what is to follow "our"?—speak, what—our journey into the country I suppose—Oh woman, damned woman! and Love, damned Love, their old tempter! for this is one of his miracles; in a moment he can make those blind that could see, and those see that were blind, those dumb that could speak, and those prattle who were dumb before; nay, what is more than all, make these dough-baked, senseless, indocile animals, women, too hard for us their politic lords and rulers, in a moment. But make an end to your letter, and then I'll make an end of you thus, and all my plagues together.

THE WONDER: A WOMAN KEEPS A SECRET
by Susanna Centlivre

Colonel Briton receives a love letter from the damsel-in-distress Isabella, who requests a secret meeting with her mysterious rescuer. With his man-servant Gibby in tow, the Colonel sets off to the appointed place of rendezvous.

COLONEL:

Well, though I could not see my fair incognita, Fortune, to make me amends, has flung another intrigue my way. Oh! how I love these pretty kind coming females that won't give a man the trouble of racking his invention to deceive them.—"Oh, Portugal! thou dear garden of pleasure—where love drops down his mellow fruit, and every bough bends to our hands, and seems to cry, 'come, pull, and eat': how deliciously a man lives here without fear of the stool of repentance!"—This letter I received from a lady in a veil—some duenna, some necessary implement of Cupid. I suppose the style is frank and easy, I hope I like her than writ it. (*Reads.*) "Sir, I have seen your person and like it,"—very concise—"and if you'll meet at four o'clock in the morning, upon the Terriero de passa, half an hour's conversation will let me into your mind."—Ha, ha, ha! a philosophical wench? This is the first time I ever knew a woman had any business with the mind of a man.—"If your intellects answer your outward appearance, the adventure may not displease you. I expect you'll not attempt to see my face, nor offer any thing unbecoming the gentleman I take you for."—Humph, the gentleman she takes me for ! I hope she takes me to be flesh and blood, and then I'm sure I shall do nothing unbecoming a gentleman. Come along then, it is pretty near the time.—I like a woman that rises early to pursue her inclination.

SIR HARRY WILDAIR
by George Farquhar

The ever frolicksome Sir Harry Wildair, having been foiled in his attempts to seduce Lady Lurewell by her watchful husband, tries his luck with Lord Bellamy's wife. The next morning Bellamy confronts the young gallant, who uses his sharp wit to talk his way out of a confession.

SIR HARRY WILDAIR:

Look ye, my Lord, don't frown; it spoils your face.—But if you must know, your lady owes me two hundred guineas, and that sum I will presume to extort from your lordship. Honour! Ha, ha, ha!—Look ye, my lord, when you and I were under the tuition of our governors, and conversed only with old Cicero, Livy, Virgil, Plutarch, and the like; why then such a man was a villain, and such a one was a man of honour: but now, that I have known the court, a little of what they call the *beau-monde* and the *bel esprit*, I find that honour looks as ridiculous as roman buskins upon your lordship, or my full peruke upon Scipio Africanus. Because the world's improved, my lord, and we find that this honour is a very troublesome and impertinent thing— Can't we live together like good neighbours and Christians, as they do in France? I lend you my coach, I borrow yours; you dine with me, I sup with you; I lie with your wife, and you lie with mine.—Honour! That's such an impertinence!—Pray, my lord, hear me. What does your honour think of murdering your friend's reputation; making a jest of his misfortunes; cheating him at cards; debauching his bed; or the like? Pish! Pish! Nothing but good manners; excess of good manners. Why you ha'n't been at court lately. There 'tis the only practice to shew our wit and breeding.—As for instance: your friend reflects upon you when absent, because 'tis good manners; rallies you when present, because 'tis witty; cheats you at piquet, to shew he has been in France; and lies with your wife, to shew he's a man of quality. In short, my lord, you have a wrong notion of things. Should a man with a handsome wife revenge all affronts done to his honour, taverns and chocolate houses could not subsist;—Come, come, my lord, no more on't, for shame; your honour is safe enough, for I have the key of its back door in my pocket.

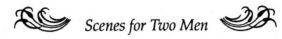

Scenes for Two Men

THE COUNTRY WIFE 🌶

by William Wycherly

Horner
Pinchwife

Mr. Pinchwife, a jealous, overbearing husband, confronts the libertine Mr. Horner for attempting to make him a cuckold with his country wife. He presents Mr. Horner with a letter he forced his wife to write. Horner assures him that his motivations were pure, and vows to obey Mrs. Pinchwife's words to the letter, which secretly defy all of Pinchwife's intentions.

HORNER:
  Well, what brings my dear friend hither?
PINCHWIFE:
  Your impertinency.
HORNER:
  My impertinency!—why, you gentlemen that have got handsome wives, think you have a privilege of saying anything to your friends, and are as brutish as if you were our creditors.
PINCHWIFE:
  No, sir, I'll ne'er trust you any way.
HORNER:
  But why not, dear Jack? why diffide in me thou know'st so well?
PINCHWIFE:
  Because I do know you so well.
HORNER:
  Han't I been always thy friend, honest Jack, always ready to serve thee, in love or battle, before thou wert married, and am so still?
PINCHWIFE:
  I believe so, you would be my second now, indeed.
HORNER:
  Well then, dear Jack, why so unkind, so grum, so strange to me? Come, prithee kiss me, dear rogue: gad, I was always, I say, and am still as much thy servant as—

PINCHWIFE:

As I am yours, sir. What, you would send a kiss to my wife, is that it?

HORNER:

So, there 'tis—a man can't show his friendship to a married man, but presently he talks of his wife to you. Prithee, let thy wife alone, and let thee and I be all one, as we were wont. What, thou art as shy of my kindness as a Lombard Street alderman of a courtier's civility at Locket's!

PINCHWIFE:

But you are overkind to me, as kind as if I were your cuckold already; yet I must confess you ought to be kind and civil to me, since I am so kind, so civil to you, as to bring you this; look you there, sir. (*Delivers him a letter.*)

HORNER:

What is't?

PINCHWIFE:

Only a love letter, sir.

HORNER:

From whom?—how! this is from your wife—hum—and hum— (*Reads.*)

PINCHWIFE:

Even from my wife, sir: am I not wondrous kind and civil to you now too?—(*Aside.*) But you'll not think her so.

HORNER:

(*Aside.*) Ha! is this a trick of his or hers?

PINCHWIFE:

The gentleman's surprised I find.—What, you expected a kinder letter?

HORNER:

No faith, not I, how could I?

PINCHWIFE:

Yes, yes, I'm sure you did. A man so well made as you are, must needs be disappointed, if the women declare not their passion at first sight or opportunity.

HORNER:

(*Aside.*) But what should this mean? Stay, the postscript. (*Reads aside.*) "Be sure you love me, whatsoever my husband says to the contrary, and let him not see this, lest he should come home

and pinch me, or kill my squirrel."—It seems he knows not what
the letter contains.

PINCHWIFE:

Come, ne'er wonder at it so much.

HORNER:

Faith, I can't help it.

PINCHWIFE:

Now, I think I have deserved your infinite friendship and kindness, and have showed myself sufficiently an obliging kind
friend and husband; am I not so, to bring a letter from my wife
to her gallant?

HORNER:

Ay, the devil take me, art thou, the most obliging, kind friend
and husband in the world, ha! ha!

PINCHWIFE:

Well, you may be merry, sir; but in short I must tell you, sir, my
honor will suffer no jesting.

HORNER:

What dost thou mean?

PINCHWIFE:

Does the letter want a comment? Then, know, sir, though I have
been so civil a husband, as to bring you a letter from my wife, to
let you kiss and court her to my face, I will not be a cuckold, sir,
I will not.

HORNER:

Thou art mad with jealousy. I never saw thy wife in my life but
at the play yesterday, and I know not if it were she or no. I court
her, kiss her!

PINCHWIFE:

I will not be a cuckold, I say; there will be danger in making me
a cuckold.

HORNER:

Why, wert thou not well cured of thy last clap?

PINCHWIFE:

I wear a sword.

HORNER:

It should be taken from thee, less thou should'st do thyself a
mischief with it; thou art mad, man.

PINCHWIFE:

As mad as I am, and as merry as you are, I must have more reason from you ere we part. I say again, though you kissed and
courted last night my wife in man's clothes, as she confesses in
her letter—

HORNER:

(*Aside.*) Ha!

PINCHWIFE:

Both she and I say, you must not design it again, for you have
mistaken your woman, as you have done your man.

HORNER:

(*Aside.*) Oh—I understand something now—(*Aloud.*) Was that
thy wife! Why would'st thou not tell me 'twas she? Faith, my
freedom with her was your fault, not mine.

PINCHWIFE:

(*Aside.*) Faith, so 'twas.

HORNER:

Fy! I'd never do't to a woman before her husband's face, sure.

PINCHWIFE:

But I had rather you should do't to my wife before my face, than
behind my back; and that you shall never do.

HORNER:

No—you will hinder me.

PINCHWIFE:

If I would not hinder you, you see by her letter she would.

HORNER:

Well, I must e'en acquiesce then, and be contented with what
she writes.

PINCHWIFE:

I'll assure you 'twas voluntarily writ; I had no hand in't you
may believe me.

HORNER:

I do believe thee, faith.

PINCHWIFE:

And I believe her too, for she's an innocent creature, has no dissembling in her: and so fare you well, sir.

HORNER:

Pray, however, present my humble service to her, and tell her I
will obey her letter to a tittle, and fulfill her desires, be what
they will, or with what difficulty soever I do't; and you shall be

no more jealous of me, I warrant her, and you.

PINCHWIFE:

Well then, fare you well; and play with any man's honor but mine, kiss any man's wife but mine, and welcome. (*Exit.*)

THE FORC'D MARRIAGE; or
THE JEALOUS BRIDEGROOM *∂*
by Aphra Behn

Philander
Alcander

Erminia had been promised in marriage to Prince Philander, but she has instead wed another, Alcippus. Erminia confesses her previous love for Philander to Alcippus on their wedding night, and manages to delay the consummation of their marriage. Suffering from what he believes is his beloved's broken promise, Philander confides his misery to his manservant Alcander.

PHILANDER:
> What's a clock, Alcander?

ALCANDER:
> 'Tis midnight, sir, will you not go to bed?

PHILANDER:
> To bed, friend; what to do?

ALCANDER:
> To sleep, sir, as you were wont to do.

PHILANDER:
> Sleep, and Erminia have abandon'd me;
> I'll never sleep again.

ALCANDER:
> This is an humour, sir, you must forsake.

PHILANDER:
> Never, never, oh Alcander.
> Dost know where my Erminia lies tonight?

ALCANDER:
> I guess, sir.

PHILANDER:
> Where? Nay, prithee speak,
> Indeed I shall not be offended at it.

ALCANDER:
> I know not why you should, sir;
> She's where she ought, abed with young Alcippus.

PHILANDER:

Thou speak'st thy real thoughts.

ALCANDER:

Why should your Highness doubt it?

PHILANDER:

By Heaven, there is no faith in woman-kind;
Alcander, dost thou know an honest woman?

ALCANDER:

Many, sir.

PHILANDER:

I do not think it, 'tis impossible;
Erminia, if it could have been, were she,
But she has broke her vows, which I held sacred,
And plays the wanton in another's arms.

ALCANDER:

Sir, do you think it just to wrong her so?

PHILANDER:

Oh, would thou couldst persuade me that I did so.
Thou know'st the oaths and vows she made to me,
Never to marry other than myself,
And you, Alcander, wrought me to believe them.
But now her vows to marry none but me,
Are given to Alcippus, and in his bosom breath'd,
With balmy whispers, whilst the ravisht youth
For every syllable returns a kiss,
And in the height of all his ecstacy,
Philander's dispossess'd and quite forgotten.
Ah, charming maid, is this your love to me?
Yet now thou art no maid, nor lov'st not me,
And I the fool to let thee know my weakness.

ALCANDER:

Why do you thus proceed to vex yourself?
To question what you list, and answer what you please?
Sir, this is not the way to be at ease.

PHILANDER:

Ah, dear Alcander, what would'st have me do?

ALCANDER:

Do that which may preserve you;
Do that which every man in love would do;

Make it your business to possess the object.

PHILANDER:

What meanest thou, is she not married?—

ALCANDER:

What then? she'as all about her that she had,
Of youth and beauty she is mistress still,
And may dispose of it how and where she will.

PHILANDER:

Pray heaven I do not think too well of thee:
What means all this discourse, art thou honest?

ALCANDER:

As most men of my age.

PHILANDER:

And wouldst thou counsel me to such a sin?
For—I do understand—thee.

ALCANDER:

I know not what you term so.

PHILANDER:

I never thought thou'dst been so great a villain,
To urge me to a crime would damn us all;
Why dost thou smile, hast thou done well in this?

ALCANDER:

I thought so, or I'ad kept it to myself.
Sir, e'er you grow in rage at what I've said,
Do you think I love you, or believe my life
Were to be valued more than your repose?
You seem to think it is not.

PHILANDER:

Possibly I may.

ALCANDER:

The sin of what I have propos'd to you
You only seem to hate: Sir, is it so?
—If such religious thoughts about you dwell,
Why is it that you thus perplex yourself?
Self-murder sure is much the greater sin.
Erminia too you say has broke her vows,
She that will swear and lie, will do the rest.
And of these evils, this I think the least;
And as for me, I never thought it sin.

PHILANDER:

    And canst thou have so poor a thought of her?

ALCANDER:

    I hope you'll find her, sir, as willing to't
    As I am to suppose it; nay, believe't,
    She'll look upon't as want of love and courage
    Should you not now attempt it;
    You know, sir, there's no other remedy,
    Take no denial, but the game pursue,
    For what she will refuse, she wishes you.

PHILANDER:

    With such pretensions—she may angry grow.

ALCANDER:

    I never heard of any that were so,
    For though the will to do't, and power they want,
    They love to hear of what they cannot grant.

PHILANDER:

    No more,
    Is this your duty to your Prince, Alcander?
    You were not wont to counsel thus amiss,
    'Tis either disrespect or some design;
    I could be wondrous angry with thee now,
    But that my grief has such possession here,
    'Twill make no room for rage.

ALCANDER:

    I cannot, sir, repent of what I've said,
    Since all the errors which I have committed
    Are what my passion to your interest led me to,
    But yet I beg your Highness would recall
    That sense which would persuade you 'tis unjust.

PHILANDER:

    Name it no more, and I'll forgive it thee.

ALCANDER:

    I can obey you, sir.

PHILANDER:

    What shall we do tonight, I cannot sleep.

ALCANDER:

    I'm good at watching, and doing anything.

PHILANDER:

We'll serenade the ladies and the bride.
Soft touches may allay the discords here,
And sweeten, though not lessen my despair.
(Exeunt.)

THE PLAIN DEALER

by William Wycherly

Freeman
Captain Manly

*Captain Manly, the "Plain Dealer," has recently returned from
fighting the Dutch at sea. Manly, distressed by the loss of his ship,
has become surly and distrustful. He is disgusted with the
hypocrisy of those around him and the "decorums" and "cere-
monies" which, in his opinion, only disguise people's contempt for
one another. He enters into a debate on the subject with his lieutenant Freeman.*

FREEMAN:

But what, will you see nobody? Not your friends?

MANLY:

Friends—I have but one, and he, I hear, is not in town; nay, can
have but one friend, for a true heart admits but of one friendship
as of one love. But in having that friend I have a thousand, for
he has the courage of men in despair, yet the diffidency and cau-
tion of cowards, the secrecy of the revengeful and the constancy
of martyrs, one fit to advise, to keep a secret, to fight and die for
his friend. Such I think him, for I have trusted him with my mistress in my absence, and the trust of beauty is sure the greatest
we can show.

FREEMAN:

Well, but all your good thoughts are not for him alone, I hope.
Pray, what d'ye think of me for a friend?

MANLY:

Of thee! Why, thou art a latitudinarian in friendship, that is, no
friend; thou dost side with all mankind but will suffer for none.
Thou art indeed like your Lord Plausible, the pink of courtesy,
therefore hast no friendship, for ceremony and great professing
renders friendship as much suspected as it does religion.

FREEMAN:

And no professing, no ceremony at all in friendship were as unnatural and as undecent as in religion; and there is hardly such a

thing as an honest hypocrite, who professes himself to be worse than he is, unless it be yourself, for though I could never get you to say you were my friend, I know you'll prove so.

MANLY:

I must confess I am so much your friend I would not deceive you, therefore must tell you, not only because my heart is taken up but according to your rules of friendship, I cannot be your friend.

FREEMAN:

Why, pray?

MANLY:

Because he that is, you'll say, a true friend to a man is a friend to all his friends. But you must pardon me, I cannot wish well to pimps, flatterers, detractors, and cowards, stiff nodding knaves and supple, pliant, kissing fools. Now, all these I have seen you use like the dearest friends in the world.

FREEMAN:

Hah, hah, hah—What, you observed me, I warrant, in the galleries of Whitehall doing the business of the place! Pshaw! Court professions, like court promises, go for nothing, man. But, faith, could you think I was a friend to all those I hugged, kissed, flattered, bowed to? Hah, ha—

MANLY:

You told 'em so and swore it too; I heard you.

FREEMAN:

Ay, but when their backs were turned did I not tell you they were rogues, villains, rascals whom I despised and hated?

MANLY:

Very fine! But what reason had I to believe you spoke your heart to me since you professed deceiving so many?

FREEMAN:

Why, don't you know, good captain, that telling truth is a quality as prejudicial to a man that would thrive in the world as square play to a cheat, or true love to a whore! Would you have a man speak truth to his ruin? You are severer than the law, which requires no man to swear against himself. You would have me speak truth against myself, I warrant, and tell my promising friend, the courtier, he has a bad memory?

MANLY:

Yes.

FREEMAN:

And so make him remember to forget my business. And I should tell the great lawyer that he takes oftener fees to hold his tongue than to speak?

MANLY:

No doubt on't.

FREEMAN:

Ay, and have him hang or ruin me, when he should come to be a judge and I before him. And you would have me tell the new officer who bought his employment lately that he is a coward?

MANLY:

Ay.

FREEMAN:

And so get myself cashiered, not him, he having the better friends though I the better sword. And I should tell the scribbler of honour that heraldry were a prettier and fitter study for so fine a gentleman than poetry?

MANLY:

Certainly.

FREEMAN:

And so find myself mauled in his next hired lampoon. And you would have me tell the holy lady too she lies with her chaplain?

MANLY:

No doubt on't.

FREEMAN:

And so draw the clergy on my back and want a good table to dine at sometimes. And by the same reason too, I should tell you that the world thinks you a madman, a brutal, and have you cut my throat, or worse, hate me! What other good success of all my plain-dealing could I have than what I've mentioned.

MANLY:

Why, first your promising courtier would keep his word, out of fear of more reproaches or at least would give you no more vain hopes. Your lawyer would serve you more faithfully, for he, having no honour but his interest, is truest still to him he knows suspects him. The new officer would provoke thee to make him a coward and so be cashiered, that thou or some other honest fellow, who had more courage than money, might get his place. The noble sonneteer would trouble thee no more with his madrigals. The praying lady would leave off railing at wenching before thee and not turn away her chambermaid for her own known frailty with thee. And I, instead of hating thee, should love thee for thy plain dealing and, in lieu of being mortified, am proud that the world and I think not well of one another.

FREEMAN:

Well, doctors differ. You are for plain dealing, I find; but against your particular notions I have the practice of the whole world. Observe but any morning what people do when they get together on the Exchange, in Westminster Hall, or the galleries of Whitehall.

MANLY:

I must confess, there they seem to rehearse Bayes's grand dance: here you see a bishop bowing low to a gaudy atheist, a judge to a doorkeeper, a great lord to a fishmonger or a scrivener with a jack chain about his neck, a lawyer to a sergeant-at-arms, a velvet physician to a threadbare chemist and a supple gentleman usher to a surly beefeater, and so tread round in a preposterous huddle of ceremony to each other, whilst they can hardly hold their solemn false countenances.

FREEMAN:

Well, they understand the world.

MANLY:

Which I do not, I confess.

FREEMAN:

But, sir, pray believe the friendship I promise you real, whatsoever I have professed to others. Try me at least.

MANLY:

Why, what would you do for me?

FREEMAN:

I would fight for you.

MANLY:

That you do for your own honour. But what else?

FREEMAN:

I would lend you money, if I had it.

MANLY:

To borrow more of me another time. That were but putting your money to interest; a usurer would be as good a friend. But what other piece of friendship?

FREEMAN:

I would speak well of you to your enemies.

MANLY:

To encourage others to be your friends by a show of gratitude.
But what else?

FREEMAN:

Nay, I would not hear you ill spoken of behind your back by my
friend.

MANLY:

Nay, then thou'rt a friend indeed. But it were unreasonable to
expect it from thee as the world goes now, when new friends,
like new mistresses, are got by disparaging old ones.

THE RECRUITING OFFICER

by George Farquhar

Plume
Worthy

Captain Plume, a recruiting officer, has just ridden thirty hours on horseback from London to Shrewsbury. Here he catches up on romantic news with his melancholic friend, Mr. Worthy, a gentleman in this small town. For all his bawdy remarks and insinuations, the rakish Plume remains true to Sylvia while resisting Melinda and other temptations in the course of the play.

PLUME:

What, arms across, Worthy! methinks you should hold them open when a friend's so near—The man has got the vapours in his ears, I believe. I must expel this melancholy spirit.
Spleen, thou worst of fiends below,
Fly, I conjure thee, by this magic blow.
(*Slaps Worthy on the shoulder.*)

WORTHY:

Plume! my dear captain! welcome. Safe and sound return'd!

PLUME:

I 'scaped safe from Germany, and sound, I hope, from London: you see I have lost neither leg, arm, nor nose. Then for my inside, 'tis neither troubled with sympathies nor antipathies; and I have an excellent stomach for roast beef.

WORTHY:

Thou art a happy fellow: once I was so.

PLUME:

What ails thee, man? no inundations nor earthquakes in Wales I hope? Has your father rose from the dead and reassumed his estate?

WORTHY:

No.

PLUME:

Then you are marry'd, surely?

WORTHY:

No.

PLUME:

Then you are mad, or turning quaker?

WORTHY:

Come, I must out with it—Your once gay roving friend is dwindled into an obsequious, thoughtful, romantic, constant coxcomb.

PLUME:

And, pray, what is all this for?

WORTHY:

For a woman.

PLUME:

Shake hands, brother. If thou go to that, behold me as obsequious, as thoughtful, and as constant a coxcomb as your worship.

WORTHY:

For whom?

PLUME:

For a regiment—but for a woman! 'Sdeath! I have been constant to fifteen at a time, but never melancholy for one: and can the love of one bring you into this condition? Pray, who is this wonderful Helen?

WORTHY:

A Helen indeed! not to be won under ten years siege; as great a beauty, and as great a jilt.

PLUME:

A jilt! pho! is she as great a whore?

WORTHY:

No, no.

PLUME:

'Tis ten thousand pities! But who is she? do I know her?

WORTHY:

Very well.

PLUME:

That's impossible—I know no woman that will hold out a ten years siege.

WORTHY:

What think you of Melinda?

PLUME:

Melinda! why she began to capitulate this time twelvemonth,

and offered to surrender upon honourable terms: and I advis'd
you to propose a settlement of five hundred pounds a-year to
her, before I went last abroad.

WORTHY:

I did, and she hearken'd to it, desiring only one week to consider—when beyond her hopes the town was reliev'd, and I
forc'd to turn my siege into a blockade.

PLUME:

Explain, explain.

WORTHY:

My lady Richly, her aunt in Flintshire, dies, and leaves her, at
this critical time, twenty thousand pounds.

PLUME:

Oh, the devil! what a delicate woman was there spoil'd. But, by
rules of war, now—Worthy, blockade was foolish—After such a
convoy of provisions was enter'd the place, you could have no
thought of reducing it by famine; you should have redoubled
your attacks, taken the town by storm, or have died upon the
breach.

WORTHY:

I did make one general assault, but was so vigorously repuls'd,
that, despairing of ever gaining her for a mistress, I have alter'd
my conduct, given my addresses the obsequious and distant
turn, and court her now for a wife.

PLUME:

So, as you grew obsequious she grew haughty, and, because you
approached her like a goddess, she us'd you like a dog.

WORTHY:

Exactly.

PLUME:

'Tis the way of 'em all—Come, Worthy, your obsequious and
distant airs will never bring you together; you must not think to
surmount her pride by your humility. Would you bring her to
better thoughts of you, she must be reduc'd to a meaner opinion
of herself. Let me see, the very first thing that I would do should
be to lie with her chambermaid, and hire three or four wenches
in the neighbourhood to report that I had got them with child—
Suppose we lampoon'd all the pretty women in town and left
her out; or, what if we made a ball, and forgot to invite her, with
one or two of the ugliest.

WORTHY:

These would be mortifications I must confess; but we live in such a precise, dull place that we can have no balls, no lampoons, no—

PLUME:

What! no bastards! and so many recruiting officers in town! I thought 'twas a maxim among them to leave as many recruits in the country as they carry'd out.

WORTHY:

Nobody doubts your goodwill, noble captain! in serving your country with your best blood, witness our friend Molly at The Castle; there have been tears in town about that business, captain.

PLUME:

I hope Sylvia has not heard of it.

WORTHY:

Oh, sir, have you thought of her? I began to fancy you had forgot poor Sylvia.

PLUME:

Your affairs had quite put mine out of my head. 'Tis true, Sylvia and I had once agreed to go to bed together, could we have adjusted preliminaries; but she would have the wedding before consummation, and I was for consummation before the wedding: we could not agree. She was a pert obstinate fool, and would lose her maidenhead her own way, so she might keep it for Plume.

WORTHY:

But do you intend to marry upon no other conditions?

PLUME:

Your pardon, sir, I'll marry upon no condition at all—If I should, I am resolv'd never to bind myself down to a woman for my whole life, till I know whether I shall like her company for half an hour. Suppose I marry'd a woman that wanted a leg— such a thing might be, unless I examined the goods beforehand—If people would but try one another's constitutions before they engag'd, it would prevent all these elopements, divorces, and the devil knows what.

WORTHY:

Nay, for that matter, the town did not stick to say that—

PLUME:

I hate country towns for that reason—If your town has a dishonourable thought of Sylvia, it deserves to be burnt to the ground—I love Sylvia, I admire her frank generous disposition—there's something in that girl more than woman—her sex is but a foil to her—the ingratitude, dissimulation, envy, pride, avarice, and vanity, of her sister females, do but set off their contraries in her—In short, were I once a general, I would marry her.

WORTHY:

Faith, you have reason—for were you but a corporal, she would marry you—But my Melinda conquets it with every fellow she sees—I'll lay fifty pounds she makes love to you.

PLUME:

I'll lay you a hundred, that I return it if she does.—Look'e, Worthy, I'll win her and give her to you afterwards.

WORTHY:

If you win her you shall wear her, faith; I would not value the conquest without the credit of the victory.

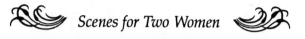 *Scenes for Two Women*

THE WAY OF THE WORLD ✦

by William Congreve

Lady Wishfort
Foible

*Lady Wishfort, bitter toward Mirabell for turning his attentions
from herself toward her niece, Millamant, is further enraged upon
hearing his slanders about her. Foible, her maidservant, provides
incentive for revenge with the news if the imminent arrival of
Mirabell's "wealthy uncle" Sir Rowland whom Lady Wishfort desires to court.*

LADY WISHFORT:

O Foible, where has thou been? what hast thou been doing?

FOIBLE:

Madam, I have seen the party.

LADY WISHFORT:

But what hast thou done?

FOIBLE:

Nay, 'tis your ladyship has done, and are to do; I have only
promised. But a man so enamoured—so transported!—Well,
here it is, all that is left; all that is not kissed away.—Well, if
worshipping of pictures be a sin—poor Sir Rowland, I say.

LADY WISHFORT:

The miniature has been counted like—but hast thou not be-
trayed me, Foible? Hast thou not detected me to that faithless
Mirabell?—What hadst thou to do with him in the Park?
Answer me, has he got nothing out of thee?

FOIBLE:

(*Aside.*) So the devil has been beforehand with me. What shall I
say?—(*Aloud.*)—Alas, madam, could I help it, if I met that confident thing? was I in fault? If you had heard how he used me,
and all upon your ladyship's account, I'm sure you would not
suspect my fidelity. Nay, if that had been the worst, I could have
borne; but he had a fling at your ladyship too; and then I could
not hold, but i'faith I gave him his own.

LADY WISHFORT:

Me? what did the filthy fellow say?

FOIBLE:

O madam! 'tis a shame to say what he said—with his taunts and his fleers, tossing up his nose. Humph! (says he) what, you are hatching some plot (says he) you are so early abroad, or catering (says he), ferreting some disbanded officer, I warrant.—Half-pay is but thin subsistence (says he)—well, what pension does your lady propose? Let me see (says he), what, she must come down pretty deep now, she's superannuated (says he) and—

LADY WISHFORT:

Odds my life, I'll have, I'll have him murdered! I'll have him poisoned! Where does he eat?—I'll marry a drawer to have him poisoned in his wine. I'll send for Robin from Locket's immediately.

FOIBLE:

Poison him! poisoning's too good for him. Starve him, madam, starve him; marry Sir Rowland and get him disinherited. Oh you would bless yourself to hear what he said!

LADY WISHFORT:

A villain! superannuated!

FOIBLE:

Humph (says he), I hear you are laying designs against me too (says he), and Mrs. Millamant is to marry my uncle (he does not suspect a word of your ladyship); but (says he) I'll fit you for that. I warrant you (says he) I'll hamper you for that (says he); you and your old frippery too (says he); I'll handle you—

LADY WISHFORT:

Audacious villain! handle me; would he durst!—Frippery! old frippery! was there ever such a foul-mouthed fellow? I'll be married tomorrow; I'll be contracted tonight.

FOIBLE:

The sooner the better, madam.

LADY WISHFORT:

Will Sir Rowland be here, sayest thou? when, Foible?

FOIBLE:

Incontinently, madam. No new sheriff's wife expects the return of her husband after knighthood with that impatience in which Sir Rowland burns for the dear hour of kissing your ladyship's hand after dinner.

LADY WISHFORT:

Frippery! superannuated frippery! I'll frippery the villain; I'll reduce him to frippery and rags! a tatterdemalion! I hope to see him hung with tatters, like a Long-lane pent-house or a gibbet thief. A slander-mouthed railer! I warrant the spendthrift prodigal's in debt as much as the million lottery, or the whole court upon a birthday. I'll spoil his credit with his tailor. Yes, he shall have my niece with her fortune, he shall.

FOIBLE:

He! I hope to see him lodge in Ludgate first, and angle into Blackfriars for brass farthings with an old mitten.

LADY WISHFORT:

Ay, dear Foible; thank thee for that, dear Foible. He has put me all out of patience. I shall never recompose my features to receive Sir Rowland with any economy of face. This wretch has fretted me that I am absolutely decayed. Look, Foible.

FOIBLE:

Your ladyship has frowned a little too rashly, indeed, madam. There are some cracks discernible in the white varnish.

LADY WISHFORT:

Let me see the glass.—Cracks, sayest thou?—why, I am arrantly flayed—I look like an old peeled wall. Thou must repair me, Foible, before Sir Rowland comes, or I shall never keep up to my picture.

FOIBLE:

I warrant you, madam, a little art once made your picture like you; and now a little of the same art must make you look like your picture. Your picture must sit for you, madam.

LADY WISHFORT:

But art thou sure Sir Rowland will not fail to come? Or will he not fail when he does come? Will he be importunate, Foible, and push? For if he should not be importunate, I shall never break decorums—I shall die with confusion, if I am forced to advance.—Oh, no, I can never advance!—I shall swoon if he should expect advances. No, I hope Sir Rowland is better bred than to put a lady to the necessity of breaking her forms. I won't be too coy, neither.—I won't give him despair—but a little disdain is not amiss; a little scorn is alluring.

FOIBLE:

A little scorn becomes your ladyship.

LADY WISHFORT:

Yes, but tenderness becomes me best—a sort of dyingness—you see that picture has a sort of a—ha, Foible? a swimmingness in the eye—yes, I'll look so—my niece affects it; but she wants features. Is Sir Rowland handsome? Let my toilet be removed—I'll dress above. I'll receive Sir Rowland here: Is he handsome? Don't answer me. I won't know; I'll be surprised, I'll be taken by surprise.

FOIBLE:

By storm, madam, Sir Rowland's a brisk man.

LADY WISHFORT:

Is he! O then he'll importune, if he's a brisk man. I shall save decorums if Sir Rowland importunes. I have a mortal terror at the apprehension of offending against decorums. Oh, I'm glad he's a brisk man. Let my things be removed, good Foible. (*Exit*.)

LOVE'S LAST SHIFT ✌🏿
by Colley Cibber

Amanda
Hillaria

*Young Worthy has just informed the virtuous Amanda that her
husband Loveless, who had abandoned her ten years before, has returned to town. Young Worthy has proposed that in order to win
Loveless back, Amanda should pose as a mistress and seduce her
husband, thereby reviving his passion for her. Amanda consults
her friend Hillaria about her plan.*

AMANDA:

My Dear, I have news for you.

HILLARIA:

I guess at it, and fain wou'd be satisfied of the particulars: Your
husband is returned, and I hear knows nothing of your being
alive: young Worthy has told me of your design upon him.

AMANDA:

"Tis that I wanted your advice in: What think you of it?

HILLARIA:

O! I admire it: Next to forgetting your husband, 'tis the best
counsel was ever given you; for under the disguise of a mistress,
you may now take a fair advantage of indulging your love; and
the little experience you have had of it already, has been just
enough not to let you be afraid of a man.

AMANDA:

Will you never leave your mad humour?

HILLARIA:

Not till my youth leaves me: Why should women affect ignorance among themselves? When we converse with men, indeed,
modesty and good breeding oblige us not to understand, what,
sometimes, we can't help thinking of.

AMANDA:

Nay, I don't think the worse of you for what you say: For 'tis observ'd, that a bragging lover, and an overshy lady, are the far-
thest from what they would seem; the one is as seldom known

to receive a favour, as the other to resist an opportunity.

HILLARIA:

Most women have a wrong sense of modesty, as some men of courage; if you don't fight with all you meet, or run from all you see, you are presently thought a coward, or an ill woman.

AMANDA:

You say true; and 'tis as hard a matter, now-a-days, for a woman to know how to converse with men, as for a man to know when to draw his sword: For many times both sexes are apt to over-act their parts: To me the rules of virtue have been ever sacred; and I am loth to break 'em by an unadvised undertaking: Therefore, dear Hillaria, help me, for I am at a loss.—Can I justify, think you, my intended design upon my husband?

HILLARIA:

As how, prithee?

AMANDA:

Why, if I court and conquer him, as a mistress, am not I accessory to his violating the bonds of marriage? For tho' I'm his wife, yet while he loves me not as such, I encourage an unlawful passion; and tho' the act be safe, yet his intent is criminal: How can I answer this?

HILLARIA:

Very easily; for if he don't intrigue with you, he will with somebody else in the meantime, and I think you have as much right to his remains as anyone.

AMANDA:

Ay! but I am assured, the love he will pretend to me is vicious: And 'tis uncertain that I shall prevent his doing worse elsewhere.

HILLARIA:

'Tis true, a certain ill ought not to be done for an uncertain good. But then again, of two evils, choose the least; and sure 'tis less criminal to let him love you as a mistress, than to let him hate you as a wife. If you succeed, I suppose you will easily forgive your guilt in the undertaking.

AMANDA:

To say truth, I find no argument yet strong enough to conquer my inclination to it. But is there no danger, think you, of his knowing me?

HILLARIA:

Not the least, in my opinion: In the first place, he confidently believes you are dead: Then he has not seen you these eight or ten years: Besides, you were not above sixteen when he left you: This, with the alteration the small-pox have made in you, (tho' not for the worse) I think, are sufficient disguises to secure you from his knowledge.

AMANDA:

Nay, and to this I may add, the considerable amendment of my fortune; for when he left me, I had only my bare jointure for a subsistence: Beside my strange manner of receiving him.—

HILLARIA:

That's what I wou'd fain be acquainted with.

AMANDA:

I expect farther instructions from Mr. Worthy every moment; then you shall know all, my Dear.

HILLARIA:

Nay, he will do you no small service: For a thief is the best thief-catcher.

AMANDA:

'Tis well.—Come, my dear, I must have your assistance.

HILLARIA:

With all my heart, I love to be at the bottom of a secret: For they say the confident of any amour, has sometimes more pleasure in the observation than in the parties concern'd in the enjoyment: But, methinks, you don't look with a good heart upon the business.

AMANDA:

I can't help a little concern in a business of such moment: For tho' my reason tells me my design must prosper; yet my fears say 'twere happiness too great. Oh! to reclaim the man I'm bound by heaven to love, to expose the folly of a roving mind, in pleasing him with what he seem'd to loath, were such a sweet revenge for slighted love, so vast a triumph of rewarded constancy, as might persuade the looser part of womankind ev'n to forsake themselves, and fall in love with virtue.

THE BEAUX' STRATAGEM 🖎
by George Farquhar

Mrs. Sullen
Dorinda

Mrs. Sullen, caught in a loveless marriage, extols the virtues of her newfound love, the disguised Archer, to her sister-in-law Dorinda. Young Dorinda has also found love—in the form of Aimwell, who has disguised himself as a gentleman.

MRS. SULLEN:
Well, sister!
DORINDA:
And well, sister!
MRS. SULLEN:
What's become of my lord?
DORINDA:
What's become of his servant?
MRS. SULLEN:
Servant! he's a prettier fellow, and a finer gentleman by fifty degrees than his master.
DORINDA:
O' my conscience, I fancy you could beg that fellow at the gallows' foot!
MRS. SULLEN:
O' my conscience I could, provided I could put a friend of yours in his room.
DORINDA:
You desired me, sister, to leave you, when you transgressed the bounds of honor.
MRS. SULLEN:
Thou dear censorious country girl! what dost mean? You can't think of the man without the bedfellow, I find.
DORINDA:
I don't find anything unnatural in that thought.
MRS. SULLEN:
How a little love and good company improves a woman! why,

child, you begin to live—you never spoke before.

DORINDA:

Because I was never spoke to. My lord has told me that I have more wit and beauty than any of my sex; and I truly begin to think the man is sincere.

MRS. SULLEN:

You're in the right, Dorinda; pride is the life of a woman, and flattery is our daily bread; and she's a fool that won't believe a man there, as much as she that believes him in anything else.— But I'll lay you a guinea that I had finer things said to me than you had.

DORINDA:

Done!—What did your fellow say to ye?

MRS. SULLEN:

My fellow took the picture of Venus for mine.

DORINDA:

But my lover took me for Venus herself.

MRS. SULLEN:

Common cant! Had my spark called me a Venus directly, I should have believed him a footman in good earnest.

DORINDA:

But my lover was upon his knees to me.

MRS. SULLEN:

And mine was upon his tiptoes to me.

DORINDA:

Mine vowed to die for me.

MRS. SULLEN:

Mine swore to die with me.

DORINDA:

Mine spoke the softest moving things.

MRS. SULLEN:

Mine had his moving things too.

DORINDA:

Mine kissed my hand ten thousand times.

MRS. SULLEN:

Mine has all that pleasure to come.

DORINDA:

Mine offered marriage.

MRS. SULLEN:

O Lard! D'ye call that a moving thing?

DORINDA:

The sharpest arrow in his quiver, my dear sister! Why, my ten thousand pounds may lie brooding here this seven years, and hatch nothing at last but some ill-natured clown like yours. Whereas, if I marry my Lord Aimwell, there will be a title, place, and precedence, the Park, the play, and the drawing-room, splendor, equipage, noise, and flambeaux. "Hey, my Lady Aimwell's servants there! Lights, lights to the stairs! My Lady Aimwell's coach put forward! Stand by, make room for her ladyship!" Are not these things moving? What! melancholy of a sudden?

MRS. SULLEN:

Happy, happy sister! your angel has been watchful for your happiness, whilst mine has slept regardless of his charge.—Long smiling years of circling joys for you, but not one hour for me! (*Weeps.*)

DORINDA:

Come, my dear, we'll talk of something else.

MRS. SULLEN:

O Dorinda! I own myself a woman, full of my sex, a gentle, generous soul—easy and yielding to soft desires; a spacious heart, where love and all his train might lodge. And must the fair apartment of my breast be made a stable for a brute to lie in?

DORINDA:

Meaning your husband, I suppose?

MRS. SULLEN:

Husband! no,—even husband is too soft a name for him. But, come, I expect my brother here tonight or tomorrow; he was abroad when my father married me; perhaps he'll find a way to make me easy.

DORINDA:

Will you promise not to make yourself easy in the meantime with my lord's friend?

MRS. SULLEN:

You mistake me, sister. It happens with us as among the men, the greatest talkers are the greatest cowards; and there's a reason for it; those spirits evaporate in prattle, which might do more mischief if they took another course.—Though, to confess the truth, I do love that fellow;—and if I met him dressed as he should be, and I undressed as I should be—look ye, sister, I have no supernatural gifts—I can't swear I could resist the temptation; though I can safely promise to avoid it; and that's as much as the best of us can do.

THE RELAPSE; or, VIRTUE IN DANGER ✎
by John VanBrugh

Amanda
Berinthea

Amanda, devoted wife to Loveless, and Berinthea, her widowed cousin, discuss the pitfalls of their sex, and Berinthea's disgust with men. Unbeknownst to either, Loveless has fallen in love with Berinthea.

AMANDA:

Now, dear, Berinthea, let me enquire a little into your affairs: for I do assure you, I am enough your friend to interest myself in everything that concerns you.

BERINTHEA:

You formerly have given me such proofs on't, I should be very much to blame to doubt it. I am sorry I have no secrets to trust you with, that I might convince you how entire a confidence I durst repose in you.

AMANDA:

Why, is it possible, that one so young and beautiful as you should live and have no secrets?

BERINTHEA:

What secrets do you mean?

AMANDA:

Lovers.

BERINTHEA:

Oh, twenty; but not one secret one amongst 'em. Lovers in this age have too much honor to do anything underhand; they do all the above board.

AMANDA:

That, now, methinks, would make me hate a man.

BERINTHEA:

But the women of the town are of another mind: for by this means a lady may, with the expense of a few coquet glances, lead twenty fools about in a string for two or three years to-gether. Whereas, if she should allow 'em greater favors, and oblige 'em to secrecy, she would not keep one of 'em a fortnight.

AMANDA:

There's something indeed in that to satisfy the vanity of a
woman, but I can't comprehend how the men find their account
in it.

BERINTHEA:

Their entertainment, I must confess, is a riddle to me. For there's
very few of 'em ever get farther than a bow and an ogle. I have
half a score for my share, who follow me all over the town; and
at the play, the park, and the church do (with their eyes) say the
violent'st things to me—but I never hear any more of 'em.

AMANDA:

What can be the reason of that?

BERINTHEA:

One reason is, they don't know how to go farther. They have
had so little practice, they don't understand the trade. But besides their ignorance, you must know there is not one of my
half-score lovers but what follows half a score mistresses. Now
their affections, being divided amongst so many, are not strong
enough for any one to make 'em pursue her to the purpose. Like
a young puppy in a warren, they have aflirt at all and catch
none.

AMANDA:

Yet they seem to have a torrent of love to dispose of.

BERINTHEA:

They have so: but 'tis like the rivers of a modern philosopher
whose works, though a woman, I have read: it sets out with a violent stream, splits in a thousand branches, and is all lost in the
sands.

AMANDA:

But do you think this river of love runs all its course without
doing any mischief? Do you think it overflows nothing?

BERINTHEA:

Oh yes, 'tis true, it never breaks into anybody's ground that has
the least fence about it; but it overflows all the commons that lie
in its way. And this is the utmost achievement of those dreadful
champions in the field of love—the beaux.

AMANDA:

But prithee, Berinthea, instruct me a little farther, for I'm so
great a novice, I am almost ashamed on't. My husband's leaving

me whilst I was young and fond threw me into that depth of discontent, that ever since I have led so private and recluse a life, my ignorance is scarce conceivable. I therefore fain would be instructed; not, heaven knows, that what you call intrigues have any charms for me: my love and principles are too well fixed. The practic part of all unlawful love is—

BERINTHEA:

Oh, 'tis abominable: but for the speculative—that we must all confess is entertaining. The conversation of all the virtuous women in the town turns upon that and new clothes.

AMANDA:

Pray be so just then to me, to believe, 'tis with a world of innocency I would enquire whether you think those women we call women of reputation do really 'scape all other men, as they do those shadows of 'em, the beaux.

BERINTHEA:

Oh, no, Amanda; there are a sort of men make dreadful work amongst 'em: men that may be called the beaux' antipathy, for they agree in nothing but walking upon two legs.

These have brains: the beaux has none.

These are in love with their mistress: the beau with himself.

They take care of her reputation: he's industrious to destroy it.

They are decent: he's a fop.

They are sound: he's rotten.

They are men: he's an ass.

AMANDA:

If this be their character, I fancy we had here e'en now a pattern of 'em both.

BERINTHEA:

His lordship and Mr. Worthy?

AMANDA:

The same.

BERINTHEA:

As for the lord, he's eminently so: and for the other, I can assure you there's not a man in town who has a better interest with the women that are worth having an interest with. But 'tis all private: he's like a back-stair minister at court, who, whilest the reputed favorites are sauntering in the bed-chamber, is ruling the roast in the closet.

AMANDA:

He answers then the opinion I had ever had of him. Heavens! what a difference there is between him and that vain, nauseous fop, Sir Novelty! (*Taking her hand.*) I must acquaint you with a secret, cousin. 'Tis not that fool alone has talked to me of love: Worthy has been tampering too: 'tis true, he has done't in vain: not all his charms or art have power to shake me. My love, my duty, and my virtue are such faithful guards, I need not fear my heart should e'er betray me. But I wonder at is this: I find I did not start at his proposal, as when it came from one whom I contemned. I therefore mention his attempt, that I may learn from you whence it proceeds that vice, which cannot change its nature, should so far change at least its shape as that the self-same crime, proposed from one, shall seem a monster gaping at your ruin, when from another it shall look so kind as though it were your friend, and never meant to harm you. Whence, think you, can this difference proceed? For 'tis not love, heaven knows.

BERINTHEA:

Oh, no. I would not for the world believe it were. But possibly, should there a dreadful sentence pass upon you to undergo the rage of both their passions, the pain you'd apprehend from on might seem so trivial to the other, the danger would not quite so much alarm you.

AMANDA:

Fy, fy, Berinthea! You would indeed alarm me, could you incline me to a thought that all the merit of mankind combined could shake that tender love I bear my husband. No, he sits triumphant in my heart, and nothing can dethrone him.

BERINTHEA:

But should he abdicate again, do you think you should preserve the vacant throne ten tedious winters more, in hopes of his return?

AMANDA:

Indeed I think I should. Though I confess, after those obligations he has to me, should he abandon me once more, my heart would grow extremely urgent with me to root him thence, and cast him out forever.

BERINTHEA:

Were I that thing they call a slighted wife, somebody should run the risk of being that thing they call—a husband.

AMANDA:

Oh, fy Berinthea! No revenge should ever be taken against a husband; but to wrong his bed is a vengeance, which of all vengeance—

BERINTHEA:

Is the sweetest—ha, ha, ha! Don't I talk madly?

AMANDA:

Madly indeed.

BERINTHEA:

Yet I'm very innocent.

AMANDA:

That I dare swear you are. I know how to make allowances for your humor: you were always very entertaining company; but I find since marriage and widowhood have shown you the world a little, you are very much improved.

BERINTHEA:

(*Aside.*) Alackaday, there has gone more than that to improve me, if she knew all.

AMANDA:

For heaven's sake, Berinthea, tell me what way I shall take to persuade you to come and live with me.

BERINTHEA:

Why, one way in the world there is—and but one.

AMANDA:

Pray which is that?

BERINTHEA:

It is to assure me—I shall be very welcome.

AMANDA:

If that be all, you shall e'en lie here tonight.

BERINTHEA:

Tonight?

AMANDA:

Yes, tonight.

BERINTHEA:

Why, the people where I lodge will think me mad.

AMANDA:

Let 'em think what they please.

BERINTHEA:

Say you so, Amanda? Why then they shall think what they please: for I'm a young widow, and I care not what anybody thinks. Ah, Amanda, it's a delicious thing to be a young widow.

AMANDA:

You'll hardly make me think so.

BERINTHEA:

Phu, because you are in love with your husband: but that is not every woman's case.

AMANDA:

I hope 'twas yours at least.

BERINTHEA:

Mine, say ye? Now have I a great mind to tell you a lie, but I should do it so awkwardly you'd find me out.

AMANDA:

Then e'en speak the truth.

BERINTHEA:

Shall I?—Then after all, I did love him, Amanda—as a nun does penance.

AMANDA:

Why did not you refuse to marry him then?

BERINTHEA:

Because my mother would have whipped me.

AMANDA:

How did you live together?

BERINTHEA:

Like man and wife—asunder;

He loved the country, I the town:

He hawks and hounds, I coaches and equipage:

He eating and drinking, I carding and playing:

He the sound of a horn, I the squeak of a fiddle.

We were dull company at table, worse abed.

Whenever we met, we gave one another the spleen.

And never agreed but once, which was about lying alone.

AMANDA:

But tell me one thing truly and sincerely.

BERINTHEA:

What's that?

AMANDA:

Notwithstanding all these jars, did not his death at last—extremely trouble you?

BERINTHEA:

Oh, yes: not that my present pangs were so very violent, but the

after-pains were intolerable. I was forced to wear a beastly
widow's band, a twelve-month for't.

AMANDA:

Women, I find, have different inclinations.

BERINTHEA:

Women, I find, keep different company. When your husband
ran away from you, if you had fallen into some of my acquaintance, 'twould have saved you many a tear. But you go and live
with a grandmother, a bishop, and an old nurse, which was
enough to make any woman break her heart for her husband.
Pray, Amanda, if ever you are a widow again, keep yourself so,
as I do.

AMANDA:

Why, do you then resolve you'll never marry?

BERINTHEA:

Oh, no; I resolve I will.

AMANDA:

How so?

BERINTHEA:

That I never may.

AMANDA:

You banter me.

BERINTHEA:

Indeed I don't. But I consider I'm a woman, and form my reso-
lutions accordingly.

AMANDA:

Well, my opinion is, form what resolution you will, matrimony
will the end on't.

BERINTHEA:

Faith, it won't.

AMANDA:

How do you know?

BERINTHEA:

I sure on't.

AMANDA:

Why, do you think 'tis impossible for you to fall in love?

BERINTHEA:

No.

AMANDA:

Nay, but to grow so passionately fond, that nothing but the man you love can give you rest?

BERINTHEA:

Well, what then?

AMANDA:

Why, then you'll marry him.

BERINTHEA:

How do you know that

AMANDA:

Why, what can you do else?

BERINTHEA:

Nothing—but sit and cry.

AMANDA:

Psha!

BERINTHEA:

Ah, poor Amanda, you have led a country life: but if you'll consult the widows of this town, they'll tell you you should never take a lease of a house you can hire for a quarter's warning.

Scenes for
One Man and One Woman

THE WAY OF THE WORLD 🍃

by William Congreve

Fainall
Mrs. Marwood

*Mr. Fainall, a fortune seeker in love with Mrs. Marwood, believes
her to be in love with Mirabell and is convinced that this will ruin
his plans for fortune. Mrs. Marwood, a willing partner in his plot,
is offended and defends her actions and threatens to expose
Fainall's deceit.*

FAINALL:
   Excellent creature! Well, sure if I should live to be rid of my
   wife, I should be a miserable man.
MRS. MARWOOD:
   Ay?
FAINALL:
   For having only that one hope, the accomplishment of it, of con-
   sequence, must put an end to all my hopes; and what a wretch is
   he who must survive his hopes! Nothing remains when that day
   comes, but to sit down and weep like Alexander when he
   wanted other worlds to conquer.
MRS. MARWOOD:
   Will you not follow'em?
FAINALL:
   Faith, I think not.
MRS. MARWOOD:
   Pray let us; I have a reason.
FAINALL:
   You are not jealous?
MRS. MARWOOD:
   Of whom?
FAINALL:
   Of Mirabell.
MRS. MARWOOD:
   If I am, is it consistent with my love to you that I am tender of
   your honor?

FAINALL:

You would intimate, then, as if there were a fellow-feeling between my wife and him.

MRS. MARWOOD:

I think she does not hate him to that degree she would be thought.

FAINALL:

But he, I fear, is too insensible.

MRS. MARWOOD:

It may be you are deceived.

FAINALL:

It may be so. I do now begin to apprehend it.

MRS. MARWOOD:

What?

FAINALL:

That I have been deceived, madam, and you are false.

MRS. MARWOOD:

That I am false! what mean you?

FAINALL:

To let you know I see through all your little arts.—Come, you both love him; and both have equally dissembled your aversion. Your mutual jealousies of one another have made you clash till you have both struck fire. I have often seen the warm confession reddening on your cheeks and sparkling from your eyes.

MRS. MARWOOD:

You do me wrong.

FAINALL:

I do not. 'Twas for my ease to oversee and willfully neglect the gross advances made him by my wife; that by permitting her to be engaged, I might continue unsuspected in my pleasures and take you oftener to my arms in full security. But could you think, because the nodding husband would not wake, that e'er the watchful lover slept?

MRS. MARWOOD:

And where withall can you reproach me?

FAINALL:

With infidelity, with loving another, with love of Mirabell.

MRS. MARWOOD:

'Tis false! I challenge you to show an instance that can confirm your groundless accusation. I hate him.

FAINALL:

And wherefore do you hate him? He is insensible and your resentment follows his neglect. An instance! the injuries you have done him are a proof: your interposing in his love. What cause had you to make discoveries of his pretended passion? to undeceive the credulous aunt, and be the officious obstacle of his match with Millamant?

MRS. MARWOOD:

My obligations to my lady urged me. I had professed a friendship to her and could not see her easy nature so abused by that dissembler.

FAINALL:

What, was it conscience then? Professed a friendship! O the pious friendships of the female sex!

MRS. MARWOOD:

More tender, more sincere, and more enduring, than all the vain and empty vows of men, whether professing love to us, or mutual faith to one another.

FAINALL:

Ha! ha! ha! you are my wife's friend too.

MRS. MARWOOD:

Shame and ingratitude! do you reproach me? you, you upbraid me? Have I been false to her, through strict fidelity to you, and sacrificed my friendship to keep my love inviolate? And have you the baseness to charge me with the guilt, unmindful of the merit? To you it should be meritorious, that I have been vicious: and do you reflect that guilt upon me which should lie buried in your bosom?

FAINALL:

You misinterpret my reproof. I meant but to remind you of the slight account you once could make of the strictest ties when set in competition with your love to me.

MRS. MARWOOD:

'Tis false; you urged it with deliberate malice! 'twas spoken in scorn, and I never will forgive it.

FAINALL:

Your guilt, not your resentment, begets your rage. If yet you loved, you could forgive a jealousy; but you are stung to find you are discovered.

MRS. MARWOOD:

It shall be all discovered. You too shall be discovered; be sure you shall. I can but be exposed.—If I do it myself I shall prevent your baseness.

FAINALL:

Why, what will you do?

MRS. MARWOOD:

Disclose it to your wife; own what has passed between us.

FAINALL:

Frenzy!

MRS. MARWOOD:

By all my wrongs I'll do't!—I'll publish to the world the injuries you have done me, both in my fame and fortune! With both I trusted you, you bankrupt in honor, as indigent of wealth.

FAINALL:

Your fame I have preserved. Your fortune has been bestowed as the prodigality of your love would have it, in pleasures which we both have shared. Yet, had not you been false, I had ere this repaid it—'tis true. Had you permitted Mirabell with Millamant to have stolen their marriage, my lady had been incensed beyond all means of reconcilement: Millamant had forfeited the moiety of her fortune, which then would have descended to my wife—and wherefore did I marry, but to make lawful prize of a rich widow's wealth, and squander it on love and you?

MRS. MARWOOD:

Deceit and frivolous pretence!

FAINALL:

Death, am I not married? What's pretence? Am I not imprisoned, fettered? Have I not a wife? nay a wife that was a widow, a young widow, a handsome widow; and would again be a widow, but that I have a heart of proof, and something of a constitution to bustle through the ways of wedlock and this world! Will you yet be reconciled to truth and me?

MRS. MARWOOD:

Impossible. Truth and you are inconsistent; I hate you and shall for ever.

FAINALL:

For loving you?

MRS. MARWOOD:

I loathe the name of love after such usage; and next to the guilt with which you would asperse me, I scorn you most. Farewell!

FAINALL:

Nay, we must not part thus.

MRS. MARWOOD:

Let me go.

FAINALL:

Come, I'm sorry.

MRS. MARWOOD:

I care not—let me go—break my hands, do—I'd leave 'em to get loose.

FAINALL:

I would not hurt you for the world. Have I no other hold to keep you here?

MRS. MARWOOD:

Well, I have deserved it all.

FAINALL:

You know I love you.

MRS. MARWOOD:

Poor dissembling!—Oh, that—well, it is not yet—

FAINALL:

What? what is it not? what is it not yet? It is not yet too late—

MRS. MARWOOD:

No, it is not yet too late—I have that comfort.

FAINALL:

It is, to love another.

MRS. MARWOOD:

But not to loathe, detest, abhor mankind, myself, and the whole treacherous world.

FAINALL:

Nay, this is extravagance.—Come, I ask your pardon—no tears—I was to blame, I could not love you and be easy in my doubts. Pray forbear—I believe you; I'm convinced I've done you wrong; and any way, every way will make amends. I'll hate my wife yet more, damn her! I'll part with her, rob her of all she's worth, and we'll retire somewhere, anywhere, to another world. I'll marry thee—be pacified.—'Sdeath, they come. Hide your face, your tears—you have a mask, wear it a moment. This way, this way—be persuaded. (*Exit.*)

THE CARELESS HUSBAND ✑

by Colley Cibber

Sir Charles
Lady Easy

Sir Charles, a careless womanizer, worried that his wife is jealous of his newly discovered affair, attempts to assuage her suspicions. Lady Easy, determined not to reveal her misgivings, wishes to make Sir Charles see her as a desirable wife.

SIR CHARLES:

My dear, how do you do? You are dressed very early today; are you going out?

LADY EASY:

Only to church, my dear.

SIR CHARLES:

Is it so late then?

LADY EASY:

The bell has just rung.

SIR CHARLES:

Well, child, how does Windsor air agree with you? Do you find yourself any better yet? or have you a mind to go to London again?

LADY EASY:

No, indeed, my dear; the air's so very pleasant that if it were a place of less company I could be content to end my days here.

SIR CHARLES:

Prithee, my dear, what sort of company would most please you?

LADY EASY:

When business would permit it, yours; and in your absence a sincere friend that were truly happy in an honest husband, to sit a cheerful hour and talk in mutual praise of our condition.

SIR CHARLES:

Are you then really very happy, my dear?

LADY EASY:

(*Smiling on him.*) Why should you question it?

SIR CHARLES:

Because I fancy I am not so good to you as I should be.

LADY EASY:

Pshah!

SIR CHARLES:

Nay, the deuce take me if I don't really confess myself so bad, that I have often wondered how any woman of your sense, rank, and person could think it worth her while to have so many useless good qualities.

LADY EASY:

Fie, my dear!

SIR CHARLES:

By my soul, I'm serious.

LADY EASY:

I can't boast of my good qualities, nor if I could, do I believe you think 'em useless.

SIR CHARLES:

Nay, I submit to you, don't you find 'em so? Do you perceive that I am one tittle the better husband for your being so good a wife?

LADY EASY:

Pshah! you jest with me.

SIR CHARLES:

Upon my life, I don't. Tell me truly, was you never jealous of me?

LADY EASY:

Did I ever give you any sign of it?

SIR CHARLES:

Um—that's true but do you really think I never gave you occasion?

LADY EASY:

That's an odd question—but suppose you had?

SIR CHARLES:

Why then, what good has your virtue done you, since all the good qualities of it could not keep me to yourself?

LADY EASY:

What occasion have you given me to suppose I have not kept you to myself?

SIR CHARLES:

I given you occasion—Fie! my dear—you may be sure I—I— look you, that is not the thing, but still a (*Aside.*) death! what a blunder have I made!—(*Aloud.*) a—still, I say, madam, you shan't make me believe you have never been jealous of me; mot that you ever had any real cause, but I know women of your principles have more pride than those that have no principles at all; and where there is pride there must be some jealousy—so that if you are jealous, my dear, you know you wrong me, and—

LADY EASY:

Why then upon my word, my dear, I don't know that I ever wronged you that way in my life.

SIR CHARLES:

But suppose I had given you a real cause to be jealous, how would you do than?

LADY EASY:

It must be a very substantial one that makes me jealous.

SIR CHARLES:

Say it were a substantial one; suppose now I were well with a woman of your own acquaintance that, under pretence of frequent visits to you, should only come to carry on an affair with me—suppose now my Lady Graveairs and I were great—?

LADY EASY:

(*Aside.*) Would I could not suppose it.

SIR CHARLES:

(*Aside.*) If I come off here I believe I am pretty safe.—Suppose I say, my lady and I were so very familiar that not only yourself, but half the town should see it?

LADY EASY:

Then I should cry myself sick in some dark closet, and forget my tears when you spoke kindly to me.

SIR CHARLES:

(*Aside.*) The most convenient piece of virtue, sure, that ever wife was mistress of.

LADY EASY:

But pray, my dear, did you ever think that I had any ill thoughts of my Lady Graveairs?

SIR CHARLES:

Oh fie! child—only you know she and I used to be a little free sometimes, so I had a mind to see if you thought there was any harm in it: but since I find you very easy, I think myself obliged to tell you that upon my soul, my dear, I have so little regard to her person, that the deuce take me if I would not as soon have an affair with thy own woman.

LADY EASY:

Indeed, my dear, I should as soon suspect you with one as t'other.

SIR CHARLES:

Poor dear—shoulds't thou?—give me a kiss!

LADY EASY:

Pshah! you don't care to kiss me.

SIR CHARLES:

By my soul I do, I wish I may die it I don't think you a very fine woman.

LADY EASY:

I only wish you would think me a good wife. (*Sir Charles kisses her.*) But pray, my dear, what has made you so strangely inquisitive?

SIR CHARLES:

Inquisitive—why—a—I don't know—one's always saying one foolish thing or another—*Toll le roll.* (*Sings and talks.*) My dear, what! are we never to have any ball here? *Toll le roll.* I fancy I could recover my dancing again, if I would but practice. *Toll loll loll.*

LADY EASY:

(*Aside.*) This excess of carelessness to me excuses half his vices: if I can make him once think seriously—time may yet be my friend. (*Exit.*)

THE ROVER; or, THE BANISH'D CAVALIERS 🌊
by Aphra Behn

Angelica
Willmore

The Englishman Willmore, "the Rover," has come to Naples in Carnival-time to make merry with his friends. He comes upon the house of the prostitute Angelica, whose picture hangs out front. Overwhelmed by her beauty and unable to pay her price—1000 crowns—Willmore pulls down the picture and so doing, inadvertently starts a brawl with others of her admirers. Angelica calls Willmore in to apologize to her, but finds her charmed by his playful innocence.

ANGELICA:
Insolent Sir, how durst you pull down my picture?
WILLMORE:
Rather, how durst you set it up, to tempt poor amorous mortals with so much excellence? which I find you have but too well consulted by the unmerciful price you set upon't.—Is all this heaven of beauty shewn to move despair in those that cannot buy? and can you think the effects of that despair shou'd be less extravagant than I have shewn?
ANGELICA:
I sent for you to ask my pardon, Sir, not to aggravate your crime.—I thought I shou'd have seen you at my feet imploring it.
WILLMORE:
You are deceived, I came to rail at you, and talk such truths, too, as shall let you see the vanity of that pride, which taught you how to set such a price on sin. For such it is, whilst that which is love's due is meanly barter'd for.
ANGELICA:
Ha, ha, ha, alas, good Captain, what pity 'tis your edifying doctrine will do no good upon me.
WILLMORE:
Tis very hard, the whole cargo or nothing—faith, Madam, my

stock will not reach it, I cannot be your chapman.—Yet I have countrymen in town, merchants of love, like me; I'll see if they put for a share, we cannot lose much by it, and what we have no use for, we'll sell upon the Friday's mart, at—Who gives more? I am studying, Madam, how to purchase you, tho at present I am unprovided of money.

ANGELICA:

Sure, this from any other man would anger me—nor shall he know the conquest he has made—Poor angry man, how I despise this railing.

WILLMORE:

Yes, I am poor—but I'm a gentleman,
And one that scorns this baseness which you practise.
Poor as I am, I would not sell my self,
No, not to gain your charming high-priz'd person.
Tho I admire you strangely for your beauty,
Yet I contemn your mind.
—And yet I wou'd at any rate enjoy you;
At your own rate—but cannot—See her
The only sum I can command on earth;
I know not where to eat when this is gone:
Yet such a slave I am to love and beauty,
This last reserve I'll sacrifice to enjoy you.
—Nay, do not frown, I know you are to be bought,
And wou'd be bought by me, by me,
For a mean trifling sum, if I could pay it down.
Which happy knowledge I will still repeat,
And lay it to my heart, it has a virtue in't,
And soon will cure those wounds your eyes have made.
—And yet—there's something so divinely powerful there—
Nay, I will gaze—to let you see my strength. (*Holds her, looks on her, and pauses and sighs.*)
By heaven, bright creature—I would not for the world
Thy fame were half so fair as is thy face. (*Turns her away from him.*)

ANGELICA:

His words go through me to the very soul. (*Aside.*)
—If you have nothing else to say to me.

WILLMORE:

Yes, you shall hear how infamous you are—
For which I do not hate thee:
But that secures my heart, and all the flames it feels
Are but so many lusts,
I know it by their sudden bold intrusion.
The fire's impatient and betrays, 'tis false—
For had it been the purer flame of love,
I should have pin'd and languish'd at your feet,
E'er found the impudence to have discover'd it.
I now dare stand your scorn, and your denial.

ANGELICA:

—Pray, tell me, Sir, are not you guilty of the same mercenary crime? When a lady is proposed to you for a wife, you never ask, how fair, discreet, or virtuous she is; but what's her fortune—which if but small, you cry—She will not do my business—and basely leave her, tho she languish for you.—Say, is not this as poor?

WILLMORE:

It is a barbarous custom, which I will scorn to defend in our sex, and do despise in yours.

ANGELICA:

Thou art a brave fellow! put up thy gold, and know,
That were thy fortune large, as is thy soul,
Thou shouldst not by my love,
Couldst thou forget those mean effects of vanity,
Which set me out to sale; and as a lover, prize
My yielding joys.
Canst thou believe they'll be entirely thine,
Without considering they were mercenary?

WILLMORE:

I cannot tell, I must bethink me first—ha, death, I'm going to believe her. (*Aside.*)

ANGELICA:

Prithee, confirm that faith—or if thou canst not—flatter me a little, 'twill please me from thy mouth.

WILLMORE:

(*Aside.*) Curse on thy charming tongue! dost thou return
My feigned ontempt with so much subtility?
Thou'st found the easiest way into my heart,

Tho I yet know that all thou say'st is false. (*Turning from her in a rage.*)

ANGELICA:

By all that's good 'tis real,

I never lov'd before, tho oft a mistress.

—Shall my first vows be slighted?

WILLMORE:

(*Aside.*) What can she mean?

ANGELICA:

(*In an angry tone.*) I find you cannot credit me.

WILLMORE:

I know you take me for an errant ass,

An ass that may be sooth'd into belief, And then be us'd at pleasure.

—But, Madam I have been so often cheated

By perjur'd, soft, deluding hypocrites,

That I've no faith left for the cozening sex,

Especially for women of your trade.

ANGELICA:

The low esteem you have of me, perhaps

May bring my heart again:

For I have Pride that yet surmounts my love. (*She turns with pride, he holds her.*)

WILLMORE:

Throw off this pride, this enemy to bliss,

And shew the power of Love: 'tis with those arms

I can be only vanquisht, made a slave.

ANGELICA:

Is all my mighty expectation vanisht?

—No, I will not hear thee talk,—thou hast a charm

In every word, that draws my heart away.

And all the thousand trophies I design'd,

Thou hast undone—Why art thou soft?

Thy looks are bravely rough, and meant for war.

Could thou not storm on still?

I then perhaps had been as free as thou.

WILLMORE:

(*Aside.*) Death! how she throws her fire about my soul!—Take heed, fair creature, how you raise my hopes,

Which once assum'd pretend to all dominion.

There's not a joy thou hast in store

I shall not then command:

For which I'll pay thee back my soul, my life.

Come, let's begin th' account this happy minute.

ANGELICA:

And will you pay me then the price I ask?

WILLMORE:

Oh, why dost thou draw me from an awful worship,

By shewing thou art no divinity?

Conceal the fiend, and shew me all the angel;

Keep me but ignorant, and I'll be devout,

And pay my vows for ever at this shrine. (*Kneels, and kisses her hand.*)

ANGELICA:

The pay I mean is but thy love for mine.

—Can you give that?

WILLMORE:

Intirely—come, let's withdraw: where I'll renew my vows,—and breathe' em with such ardour, thou shalt not doubt my zeal.

ANGELICA:

Thou hast a power too strong to be resisted. (*Exit.*)

THE CARELESS HUSBAND 🖋

by Colley Cibber

Sir Charles
Lady Easy

*Sir Charles, caught by his wife Lady Easy in one of his several in-
discretions with his wife's maidservant, asks forgiveness for his
heedless wrongs. Recognizing Sir Charles' genuine love for her,
Lady Easy demonstrates her exceptional goodwill in accepting his
apology.*

SIR CHARLES:
  Sit still, my dear,—I came to talk with you, and—which you
  may well wonder at—what I have to say is of importance, too,
  but 'tis in order to my hereafter always talking kindly to you.
LADY EASY:
  Your words were never disobliging, nor can I charge you with a
  look that ever had the appearance of unkind.
SIR CHARLES:
  The perpetual spring of your good humor lets me draw no merit
  from what I have appeared to be, which makes me curious now
  to know your thoughts of what I really am: and never having
  asked you this before, it puzzles me; nor can I (my strange negligence considered) reconcile to reason your first thoughts of venturing upon marriage with me.
LADY EASY:
  I never thought it such an hazard.
SIR CHARLES:
  How could a woman of your restraint and principles, sedate-
  ness, sense, and tender disposition, propose to see an happy life
  with one (now I reflect) that hardly took an hour's pains ev'n before marriage, to appear but what I am?—a loose, unheeding
  wretch, absent in all I do, civil, and as often rude without design, unseasonably thoughtful, easy to a fault, and, in my best of
  praise, but carelessly good-natured. How shall I reconcile your
  temper with having made so strange a choice?
LADY EASY:

Your own words may answer you—your having never seemed to be but what you really were; and through that carelessness of temper there still shone forth to me an undesigning honesty I always doubted of in smoother faces. Thus, while I saw you took least pains to win me, you pleased and wooed me most: nay, I have often thought that such a temper could never be deliberately unkind, or, at the worst, I knew that errors from want of thinking might be borne, at least when probably one moment's serious thought would end 'em. These were my worst of fears, and these, when weighed by growing love against my solid hopes, were nothing.

SIR CHARLES:

My dear, your understanding startles me, and justly calls my own in question. I blush to think I've worn so bright a jewel in my bosom and till this hour have scarce been curious once to look upon its lustre.

LADY EASY:

You set too high a value on the common qualities of an easy wife.

SIR CHARLES:

Virtues, like benefits, are double, when concealed: and I confess I yet suspect you of an higher value far than I have spoke you.

LADY EASY:

I understand you not.

SIR CHARLES:

I'll speak more plainly to you. Be free and tell me—where did you leave this handkerchief?

LADY EASY:

Hah!

SIR CHARLES:

What is't you start at? You hear the question.

LADY EASY:

What shall I say? my fears confound me.

SIR CHARLES:

Be not concerned, my dear: be easy on the truth, and tell me.

LADY EASY:

I cannot speak—and I could wish you'd not oblige me to it—'tis the only thing I ever yet refused you—and though I want a reason for my will, let me not answer you.

SIR CHARLES:

Your will then be a reason, and since I see you are so generously tender of reproaching me, 'tis fit I should be easy in my gratitude, and make what ought to be my shame my joy; let me be therefore pleased to tell you now, your wondrous conduct has waked me to a sense of your disquiet past, and resolution never to disturb it more. And (not that I offer it as a merit, but yet in blind compliance to my will) let me beg you would immediately discharge your woman.

LADY EASY:

Alas! I think not of her. (*Weeping.*) Oh, my dear! distract me not with this excess of goodness.

SIR CHARLES:

Nay, praise me not, lest I reflect how little I have deserved it. I see you are in pain to give me this confusion; come, I will not shock your softness by my untimely blush for what is past, but rather soothe you to a pleasure at my sense of joy for my recovered happiness to come. Give then to my new-born love what name you please, it cannot, shall not, be too kind—oh, it cannot be too soft for what my soul swells up with emulation to deserve. Receive me then entire at last, and take what yet no woman ever truly had, my conquered heart.

LADY EASY:

Oh, the soft treasure! Oh, the dear reward of long, desiring love!—now I am blest indeed to see you—kind without th' expense of pain in being so, to make you mine with easiness. Thus, to have you mine is something more than happiness, 'tis double life, and madness of abounding joy. But 'twas a pain intolerable to give you a confusion.

SIR CHARLES:

Oh, thou engaging virtue! But I'm too slow in doing justice to thy love: I know thy softness will refuse me, but I remember I insist upon it—let thy woman be discharged this minute.

LADY EASY:

No, my dear, think me not so low in faith, to fear that, after what you've said, 'twill ever be in her power to do me future injury. When I can conveniently provide for her I'll think on't: but to discharge her now might let her guess at the occasion, and methinks I would have all our differences, like our endearments, be equally a secret to our servants.

SIR CHARLES:

Still my superior in every way!—be it as you have better thought. Well, my dear, now I'll confess a thing that was not in your power to accuse me of; to be short, I own this creature is not the only one I have been to blame with.

LADY EASY:

I know she is not, and was always less concerned to find it so, for constancy in errors might have been fatal to me.

SIR CHARLES:

(Surprised.) What is't you know, my dear?

LADY EASY:

Come, I am not afraid to accuse you now—my Lady Graveairs. Your carelessness, my dear, let all the world know it, and it would have been hard indeed had it only been to me a secret.

SIR CHARLES:

My dear, I'll ask no more questions, for fear of being more ridiculous: I do confess I thought my discretion there had been a masterpiece. How contemptible must I have looked all this while!

LADY EASY:

You shan't say so.

SIR CHARLES:

Well, to let you see I had some shame as well as nature in me, I had writ this to my Lady Graveairs, upon my first discovering that you knew I had wronged you: read it.

LADY EASY:

(Reads.) "Something has happened that prevents the visit I intended you, and I could gladly wish you never would reproach me if I tell you 'tis utterly inconvenient that I should ever see you more." This, indeed, was more than I had merited.

SIR CHARLES:

My dear, I'm thinking there may be other things my negligence may have wronged you in; but be assured, as I discover 'em all shall be corrected. Is there any part or circumstance in your fortune that I can change or yet make easier to you?

LADY EASY:

None, my dear; your good nature never stinted me in that, and now, methinks, I have less occasion there than ever.

SIR CHARLES:

Thou easy sweetness!—Oh, what a waste on thy neglected love

has my unthinking brain committed! But time and future thrift
of tenderness shall yet repair it all: the hours will come when
this soft gliding stream that swells my heart uninterrupted shall
renew its course,
And like the ocean after ebb, shall move
With constant force of due returning love.

THE ROVER; or, THE BANISH'D CAVALIERS 🪶
by Aphra Behn

Willmore
Hellena

Hellena and her sisters have disguised themselves in costumes in order to temporarily escape the tyranny of their brother Don Pedro and enjoy Carnival-time in Naples. Hellena, a precocious young woman whom Don Pedro has "designed for a nun" against her wishes, sets out in search of a husband and settles on Willmore, "the Rover." At their first meeting, Hellena flirts outrageously with Willmore behind the safety of her mask, and arranges to meet him again in the evening, provided he stays true to her in the meantime. That night she overhears him talking about his afternoon tryst with the prostitute Angelica, and boldly, though playfully, confronts him.

WILLMORE:
A mischief on thee for putting her into my thoughts; I had quite forgot her else, and this night's debauch had drunk her quite down.

HELLENA:
Had it so, good captain? (*Claps him on the back.*)

WILLMORE:
Ha! I hope she did not hear.

HELLENA:
What, afraid of such a champion!

WILLMORE:
Oh! you're a fine lady of your word, are you not? to make a man languish a whole day—

HELLENA:
In tedious search of me.

WILLMORE:
Egad, child, thou'rt in the right, hadst thou seen what a melancholy dog I have been ever since I was a lover, how I have walkt the streets like a *Capuchin*, with my hands in my sleeves—faith, sweetheart, thou wouldst pity me.

HELLENA:

Now, if I should be hang'd, I can't be angry with him, he dissembles so heartily—Alas, good captain, what pains you have taken—Now were I ungrateful not to reward so true a servant.

WILLMORE:

Poor soul! that's kindly said, I see thou bearest a conscience—come then for a beginning shew me thy dear face.

HELLENA:

I'm afraid, my small acquaintance, you have been staying that swinging stomach you boasted of this morning; I remember then my little collation would have gone down with you, without the sauce of a handsome face—Is your stomach so queasy now?

WILLMORE:

Faith long lasting, child, spoils a man's appetite—yet if you durst treat, I could so lay about me still.

HELLENA:

And would you fall to, before a priest says grace?

WILLMORE:

Oh fie, fie, what an old out-of-fashion'd thing hast thou nam'd? Thou could'st not dash me more out of countenance, shouldst thou shew me an ugly face.

HELLENA:

You see, captain, how willing I am to be friends with you, till time and ill-luck make us lovers; and ask you the question first, rather than put your modesty to the blush, by asking me: for alas, I know you captains are such strict men, severe observers of your vows to chastity, that 'twill be hard to prevail with your tender conscience to marry a young willing maid.

WILLMORE:

Do not abuse me, for fear I should take thee at thy word, and marry thee indeed, which I'm sure will be revenge sufficient.

HELLENA:

O' my conscience, that will be our destiny, because we are both of one humour; I am as inconstant as you, for I have considered, captain, that a handsome woman has a great deal to do whilst her face is good, for then is our harvest-time to gather friends; and should I in these days of my youth, catch a fit of foolish constancy, I were undone; 'tis loitering by day-light in our great journey: therefore declare, I'll allow but one year for love, one year for indifference, and one year for hate—and then—go hang your self—for I profess myself the gay, the kind, and the inconstant the devil's in't if this won't please you.

WILLMORE:

Oh most damnably!—I have a heart with a hole quite thro it too, no prison like mine to keep a mistress in.

HELLENA:

Well, I see our business as well as humours are alike, yours to cozen as many maids as will trust you, and I as many men as have faith—See if I have not as desperate a lying look, as you can have for the heart of you. (*Pulls off her vizard; he starts.*) How do you like it, Captain?

WILLMORE:

Like it! by heav'n, I never saw so much beauty. Oh the charms of those sprightly black eyes, that strangely fair face, full of smiles and dimples! those soft round melting cherry lips! and small even white teeth! not to be exprest, but silently adored!—Oh one look more, and strike me dumb, or I shall repeat nothing else till I am mad. (*He seems to court her to pull off her vizard: she refuses.*)

HELLENA:

Tell me what did you in yonder house, and I'll unmasque.

WILLMORE:

Yonder house—oh—I went to—a—to—why, there's a friend of mine lives there.

HELLENA:

What a she, or a he friend?

WILLMORE:

A man upon my honour! a man—A she friend! no, no, madam, you have done my business, I thank you.

HELLENA:

And was't your man friend, that had more darts in's eyes than Cupid carries in a whole budget of arrows?

WILLMORE:

So—

HELLENA:

Ah such a *Bona Roba*: to be in her arms is lying in *Fresco*, all perfume air about me—Was this your man friend too?

WILLMORE:

So—

HELLENA:

That gave you the he, and the she—gold, that begets young pleasures.

WILLMORE:

Well, well, madam, then you see there are ladies in the world, that will not be cruel—there are, madam, there are—

HELLENA:

And there be men too as fine, wild, inconstant fellows as yourself, there be, captain, there be, if you go to that now—therefore I'm resolved—

WILLMORE:

Oh!

HELLENA:

To see your face no more—

WILLMORE:

Oh!

HELLENA:

Till tomorrow.

WILLMORE:

Egad you frighted me.

HELLENA:

Nor then neither, unless you'll swear never to see that lady more.

WILLMORE:

See her! why! never to think of womankind again?

HELLENA:

Kneel, and swear. (*Kneels, she gives him her hand.*)

WILLMORE:

I do, never to think—to see—to love—nor lie with any but thy self.

HELLENA:

Kiss the book.

WILLMORE:

Oh, most religiously. (*Kiss her hand.*)

HELLENA:

Now what a wicked creature am I, to damn a proper fellow.

WILLMORE:

'Twill be an age till tomorrow,—and till then I will most impatiently expect you—Adieu, my dear pretty angel. (*Exit.*)

THE COUNTRY WIFE

by William Wycherly

Pinchwife
Mrs. Pinchwife

*Mrs. Pinchwife, a country wife brought to London by her overpro-
tective husband, attempts to free herself from her husband
Pinchwife's confining demands. While seeming to obey her husband, she underhandedly exerts some of her own will in writing to
the rakish Mr. Horner whom she met at a play.*

PINCHWIFE:
Come, minx, sit down and write.
MRS. PINCHWIFE:
Ay, dear bud, but I can't do't very well.
PINCHWIFE:
I wish you could not at all.
MRS. PINCHWIFE:
But what should I write for?
PINCHWIFE:
I'll have you write a letter to your lover.
MRS. PINCHWIFE:
Oh lord, to the fine gentleman a letter!
PINCHWIFE:
Yes, to the fine gentleman.
MRS. PINCHWIFE:
Lord, you do but jeer: sure you jest.
PINCHWIFE:
I am not so merry: come, write as I bid you.
MRS. PINCHWIFE:
What, do you think I am a fool?
PINCHWIFE:
(*Aside.*) She's afraid I would not dictate any love to him, there-
fore she's unwilling.—(*Aloud.*) But you had best begin.
MRS. PINCHWIFE:
Indeed, and indeed, but I won't, so I won't.
PINCHWIFE:
Why?

MRS. PINCHWIFE:

Because he's in town; you may send for him if you will.

PINCHWIFE:

Very well, you would have him brought to you; is it come to this? I say, take the pen and write, or you'll provoke me.

MRS. PINCHWIFE:

Lord, what d'ye make a fool of me for? Don't I know that letters are never writ but from the country to London, and from London into the country? Now he's in town, and I am in town too; therefore I can't write to him, you know.

PINCHWIFE:

(*Aside*.) So, I am glad it is no worse; she is innocent enough yet.—(*Aloud*.) Yes, you may, when your husband bids you, write letters to people that are in town.

MRS. PINCHWIFE:

Oh, may I so? then I'm satisfied.

PINCHWIFE:

Come, begin: (*Dictates*.)—"Sir"—

MRS. PINCHWIFE:

Shan't I say "Dear Sir?"—You know one says always something more than bare "Sir."

PINCHWIFE:

Write as I bid you, or I will write whore with this penknife in your face.

MRS. PINCHWIFE:

Nay, good bud (*Writes*.)—"Sir"—

PINCHWIFE:

"Though I suffered last night your nauseous, loathed kisses and embraces"—Write!

MRS. PINCHWIFE:

Nay, why should I say so? You know I told you he had a sweet breath.

PINCHWIFE:

Write!

MRS. PINCHWIFE:

Let me but put out "loathed."

PINCHWIFE:

Write, I say!

MRS. PINCHWIFE:

Well then. (*Writes*.)

PINCHWIFE:

　Let's see, what have you writ?—(*Takes the paper and reads.*)
　"Though I have suffered last night your kisses and embraces"—
　Thou impudent creature! where is "nauseous" and "loathed?"

MRS. PINCHWIFE:

　I can't abide to write such filthy words.

PINCHWIFE:

　Once more write as I'd have you, and question it not, or I will
　spoil thy writing with this. I will stab out those eyes that cause
　my mischief. (*Holds up the penknife.*)

MRS. PINCHWIFE:

　Oh lord! I will.

PINCHWIFE:

　So—so—let's see now.—(*Reads.*) "Though I suffered last night
　your nauseous, loathed kisses and embraces"—go on—"yet I
　would not have you presume that you shall ever repeat them"—
　so—(*She writes.*)

MRS. PINCHWIFE:

　I have writ it.

PINCHWIFE:

　On, then—"I then concealed myself from your knowledge, to
　avoid your insolencies."—(*She writes.*)

MRS. PINCHWIFE:

　So—

PINCHWIFE:

　"The same reason, now I am out of your hands"—(*She writes.*)

MRS. PINCHWIFE:

　So—

PINCHWIFE:

　"Makes me own to you my unfortunate, though innocent, of
　being in man's clothes."—(*She writes.*)

MRS. PINCHWIFE:

　So—

PINCHWIFE:

　"That you may for evermore cease to pursue her, who hates and
　detests you"—(*She writes on.*)

MRS. PINCHWIFE:

　So—heigh! (*Sighs.*)

PINCHWIFE:

　What, do you sigh? "—detests you—as much as she loves her

husband and her honor."

MRS. PINCHWIFE:

I vow, husband, he'll ne'er believe I should write such a letter.

PINCHWIFE:

What, he'd expect a kinder from you? Come, now your name only.

MRS. PINCHWIFE:

What, shan't I say "Your most faithful humble servant till death?"

PINCHWIFE:

No, tormenting fiend!—(*Aside.*) Her style, I find, would be very soft.—(*Aloud.*) Come, wrap it up now, whilst I go fetch wax and a candle; and write on the backside, "For Mr. Horner." (*Exit.*)

MRS. PINCHWIFE:

"For Mr. Horner."—So, I am glad he has told me his name. Dear Mr. Horner! but why should I send thee such a letter that will vex thee, and make thee angry with me?—Well, I will not send it.—Ay, but then my husband will kill me—for I see plainly he won't let me love Mr. Horner—but what care I for my husband?—I won't, so I won't, send poor Mr. Horner such a letter— But then my husband—but oh, what if I writ at bottom my husband made me write it?—Ay, but then my husband would see't—Can one have no shift? ah, a London woman would have a hundred presently. Stay—what if I should write a letter, and wrap it up like this, and write upon't too? Ay, but then my husband would see't—I don't know what to do.—But yet evads I'll try, so I will—for I will not send this letter to poor Mr. Horner, come what will on't.

"Dear sweet Mr. Horner"—(*Writes and repeats what she writes.*)— so—"my husband would have me send you a base, rude, unmannerly letter; but I won't"—so—"and would have me forbid you loving me; but I won't"—so—"and would have me say to you, I hate you, poor Mr. Horner; but I won't tell a lie for him"—there—"for I'm sure if you and I were in the country at cards together"—so—"I could not help treading on your toe under the table"—so—"or rubbing knees with you, and staring in your face, till you saw me"—very well—"and then looking down, and blushing for an hour together"—so—"but I must make haste before my husband comes: and now he has taught me to write letters, you shall have the longer ones from me, who am, dear, dear, poor, dear Mr. Horner, your most humble friend, and servant to command till death—Margery Pinchwife."

Stay, I must give him a hint at bottom—so—now wrap it up just like t'other—so—now write "For Mr. Horner"—But oh now, what shall I do with it? for here comes my husband. (*Enter Pinchwife.*)

PINCHWIFE:

(*Aside.*) I have been detained by a sparkish coxcomb who pretended a visit to me; but I fear 'twas to my wife—(*Aloud.*) What, have you done?

MRS. PINCHWIFE:

Ay, ay, bud, just now.

PINCHWIFE:

Let's see't: What d'ye tremble for? what, you would not have it go?

MRS. PINCHWIFE:

Here—(*Aside.*) No, I must not give him that: so I had been served if I had given him this. (*He opens and reads the first letter.*)

PINCHWIFE:

Come, where's the wax and seal?

MRS. PINCHWIFE:

(*Aside.*) Lord, what shall I do now? Nay, then I have it—(*Aloud.*) Pray let me see't. Lord, you will think me so arrant a fool, I cannot seal a letter; I will do't, so I will. (*Snatches the letter from him, changes it for the other, seals it, and delivers it to him.*)

PINCHWIFE:

Nay, I believe you will learn that, and other things, too, which I would not have you.

MRS. PINCHWIFE:

So, han't I done it curiously?—(*Aside.*) I think I have; there's my letter going to Mr. Horner, since he'll needs have me send letters to folks.

PINCHWIFE:

'Tis very well; but I warrant, you would not have it go now?

MRS. PINCHWIFE:

Yes, indeed, but I would, bud, now.

PINCHWIFE:

Well, you are a good girl then. Come, let me lock you up in your chamber, till I come back; and be sure you come not within three strides of the window when I am gone, for I have a spy in the street.—(*Exit Mrs. Pinchwife, Pinchwife locks the door.*) At least, 'tis fit she thinks so. If we do not cheat women, they'll cheat us, and fraud may be justly used with secret enemies, of which a wife is the most dangerous; and he that has a handsome one to keep, and a frontier town, must provide against treachery, rather than open force. Now I have secured all within, I'll deal with the foe without, with false intelligence. (*Holds up the letter. Exit.*)

THE MAN OF MODE 🌿

by George Etherege

Dorimant
Harriet

*Dorimant, a notorious womanizer, has heard tell of the beauty of
Harriet, a witty, headstrong young woman. At their first meeting
in the park, Harriet rebuffs Dorimant's advances, but she is
nonetheless attracted to him. At this, their second meeting, they
engage in conversation at a party. Harriet has fallen for Dorimant,
but refuses to play the game his way; Dorimant, although loathe to
admit it, realizes that he has met his match.*

DORIMANT:

(*He bows to Harriet; she curtsies. To Harriet.*) That demure curtsy is
not amiss in jest, but do not think in earnest it becomes you.

HARRIET:

Affectation is catching, I find. From your grave bow I got it.

DORIMANT:

Where had you all that scorn and coldness in your look?

HARRIET:

From nature, sir—pardon my want of art. I have not learnt those
softness and languishing which now in faces are so much in
fashion.

DORIMANT:

You need 'em not. You have a sweetness of your own, if you
would but calm your frowns and make it settle.

HARRIET:

My eyes are wild and wandering like my passions, and cannot
yet be tied to rules of charming.

DORIMANT:

Women, indeed, have commonly a method of managing those
messengers of love. Now they will look as if they would kill,
and anon they will look as if they were dying. They point and
rebate their glances, the better to invite us.

HARRIET:

I like this variety well enough, but hate the set face that always looks as it would say, "Come love me"—a woman who at plays makes the *doux yeux* to a whole audience and at home cannot forbear 'em to her monkey.

DORIMANT:

Put on a gentle smile and let me see how well it will become you.

HARRIET:

I am sorry my face does not please you as it is, but I shall not be complaisant and change it.

DORIMANT:

Though you are obstinate, I know 'tis capable of improvement, and shall do you justice, madam, if I chance to be at court when the critics of the circle pass their judgment—for thither you must come.

HARRIET:

And expect to be taken in pieces, have all my features examined, every motion censured, and on the whole be condemned to be but pretty—or a beauty of the lowest rate. What think you?

DORIMANT:

The women—nay, the very lovers who belong to the drawing room—will maliciously allow you more than that. They always grant what is apparent, that they may the better be believed when they name concealed faults they cannot easily be disproved in.

HARRIET:

Beauty runs as great a risk exposed at court as wit does on the stage, where the ugly and the foolish all are free to censure.

DORIMANT:

(*Aside.*) I love her and dare not let her know it. I fear she has an ascendant o'er me and may revenge the wrongs I have done her sex. (*To her.*) Think of making a party, madam; love will engage.

HARRIET:

You make me start! I did not think to have heard love from you.

DORIMANT:

I never knew what 'twas to have a settled ague yet, but now and then have had irregular fits.

HARRIET:

Take heed, sickness after long health is commonly more violent and dangerous.

DORIMANT:

(*Aside.*) I have took the infection from her and feel the disease now spreading in me. (*To her.*) Is the name of love so frightful that you dare not stand it?

HARRIET:

'Twill do little execution out of your mouth on me, I am sure.

DORIMANT:

It has been fatal—

HARRIET:

To some easy women, but we are not all born to one destiny. I was informed you use to laugh at love, and not make it.

DORIMANT:

The time has been, but now I must speak—

HARRIET:

If it be on that idle subject, I will put on my serious look, turn my head carelessly from you, drop my lip, let my eyelids fall and hang half o'er my eyes—thus, while you buzz a speech of an hour long in my ear and I answer never a word. Why do you not begin?

DORIMANT:

That the company may take notice how passionately I make advances of love and how disdainfully you receive 'em.

HARRIET:

When your love's grown strong enough to make you bear being laughed at, I'll give you leave to trouble me with it. Till when, pray forbear, sir.

THE PLAIN DEALER

by William Wycherly

Captain Manly
Fidelia

Captain Manly has just discovered that his "faithful" mistress Olivia has married another man while he was at sea, and has also absconded with the money Manly had left in her care. In spite of her cruelty, he still loves her, but fears for his honor if anyone should discover that the "Plain Dealer" has become a hypocrite. Fidelia, who had disguised herself as a man in order to follow her beloved Manly to sea, appears and offers herself to him as a servant, still in disguise. He seizes the opportunity, and, much to Fidelia's dismay, sends the "young volunteer" to plead his case with Olivia.

MANLY:

How hard it is to be an hypocrite!
At least to me, who am but newly so.
I thought it once a kind of knavery,
Nay, cowardice, to hide one's faults; but now
The common frailty, love, becomes my shame.
He must not know I love th'ungrateful still,
Lest he contemn me more than she, for I,
It seems, can undergo a woman's scorn
But not a man's—
(*Enter to him Fidelia.*)

FIDELIA:

Sir, good sir, generous captain.

MANLY:

Prithee, kind impertinence, leave me. Why shouldst thou follow me, flatter my generosity now, since thou know'st I have no money left? If I had it, I'd give it thee, to buy my quiet.

FIDELIA:

I never followed yet, sir, reward or fame but you alone, nor do I now beg anything but leave to share your miseries. You should not be a niggard of 'em, since methinks you have enough to spare. Let me follow you now because you hate me, as you have often said.

MANLY:

I ever hated a coward's company, I must confess.

FIDELIA:

Let me follow you till I am none then, for you, I'm sure, will through such worlds of dangers that I shall be inured to 'em; nay, I shall be afraid of your anger more than danger and so turn valiant out of fear. Dear captain, do not cast me off till you have tried me once more. Do not, do not go to sea again without me.

MANLY:

Thou to sea! To court, thou fool. Remember the advice I gave thee; thou art a handsome spaniel and canst fawn naturally. Go, busk about and run thyself into the next great man's lobby; first fawn upon the slaves without and then run into the lady's bedchamber; thou may'st be admitted at last to tumble her bed. Go seek, I say, and lose me, for I am not able to keep thee; I have not bread for myself.

FIDELIA:

Therefore I will not go, because then I may help and serve you.

MANLY:

Thou!

FIDELIA:

I warrant you, sir, for at worst I could beg or steal for you.

MANLY:

Nay, more bragging! Dost thou not know there's venturing your life in stealing? Go, prithee, away. Thou art as hard to shake off as that flattering effeminating mischief, love.

FIDELIA:

Love, did you name? Why you are not so miserable as to be yet in love, sure!

MANLY:

No, no, prithee away, be gone, on—(*Aside.*) I had almost discovered my love and shame. Well, if I had? That thing could not think the worst of me—or if he did?—No—yes, he shall know it—he shall—but then I must never leave him, for they are such secrets that make parasites and pimps lords of their masters, for any slavery or tyranny is easier than love's.—Come hither. Since thou art so forward to serve me, hast thou but resolution enough to endure the torture of a secret? For such to some is insupportable.

FIDELIA:

I would keep it as safe as if your dear precious life depended on't.

MANLY:

Damn your dearness. It concerns more than my life, my honour.

FIDELIA:

Doubt it not, sir.

MANLY:

And do not discover it by too much fear of discovering it, but have a great care you let not Freeman find it out.

FIDELIA:

I warrant you, sir. I am already all joy with the hopes of your commands and shall be all wings in the execution of 'em. Speak quickly, sir.

MANLY:

You said you would beg for me.

FIDELIA:

I did, sir.

MANLY:

Then you shall beg for me.

FIDELIA:

With all my heart, sir.

MANLY:

That is, pimp for me.

FIDELIA:

How, sir?

MANLY:

D'ye start? Thinkst thou, thou couldst do me any other service? Come, no dissembling honour. I know you can do it handsomely; thou wert made for't. You have lost your time with me at sea; you must recover it.

FIDELIA:

Do not, sir, beget yourself more reasons for your aversion to me and make my obedience to you a fault. I am the unfittest in the world to do you such a service.

MANLY:

Your cunning arguing against it shows but how fit you are for it. No more dissembling. Here, I say, you must go use it for me to

Olivia.

FIDELIA:

To her, sir?

MANLY:

Go flatter, lie, kneel, promise, anything to get her for me. I cannot live unless I have her. Didst thou not say thou wouldst do anything to save my life? And she said you had a persuading face.

FIDELIA:

But did you not say, sir, your honour was dearer to you than your life? And would you have me contribute to the loss of that and carry love from you to the most infamous, most false and—

MANLY:

And most beautiful! (*Sighs aside.*)

FIDELIA:

Most ungrateful woman that ever lived, for sure she must be so that could desert you so soon, use you so basely, and so lately too. Do not, do not forget it, sir, and think—

MANLY:

No, I will not forget it but think of revenge. I will lie with her, out of revenge. Go, be gone, and prevail for me or never see me more.

FIDELIA:

You scorned her last night.

MANLY:

I know not what I did last night. I dissembled last night.

FIDELIA:

Heavens!

MANLY:

Be gone, I say, and bring me love or compliance back, or hopes at least, or I'll never see thy face again. By—

FIDELIA:

O do not swear, sir. First hear me.

MANLY:

I am impatient. Away. You'll find me here till twelve. (*Turns away.*)

FIDELIA:

Sir—

MANLY:

Not one word, no insinuating argument more or soothing per-

suasion; you'll have need of all your rhetoric with her. Go, strive
to alter her, not me. Be gone.

(*Exit Manly at the end of the stage.*)

FIDELIA:

Should I discover to him now my sex
And lay before him his strange cruelty,
'Twould but incense it more.—No, 'tis not time.
For his love, must I then betray my own?
Were ever love or chance, till now, severe?
Or shifting woman posed with such a task?
Forced to beg that which kills her if obtained
And give away her lover not to lose him. (*Exit Fidelia.*)

THE MAN OF MODE

by George Etherege

Mrs. Loveit
Dorimant

*The notorious womanizer Dorimant has devised a plan to rid him-
self of the the affections of his clingy, hot-tempered mistress Mrs.
Loveit. Dorimant sends his newest conquest to tell Loveit that he
was seen at the theatre courting someone else, a story which
arouses Loveit's jealous passions to the point where she sends
Dorimant away of her own accord. In an attempt to plague her
further, Dorimant encourages the silly Sir Fopling Flutter to make
advances on his former mistress. Loveit turns the tables and
openly makes love to the fop to revenge herself on Dorimant. To
save face, Dorimant pays Loveit a visit and makes her own up to
her real feelings.*

MRS. LOVEIT:

Oh, that my love would be but calm awhile, that I might receive
this man with all the scorn and indignation he deserves.
(*Enter Dorimant.*)

DORIMANT:

Now for a touch of Sir Fopling to begin with.—Hey, page! Give
positive order that none of my people stir. Let the *canaille* wait,
as they should do.—Since noise and nonsense have such powerful charms,

"I, that I may successful prove,

Transform myself to what you love."

MRS. LOVEIT:

If that would do, you need not change from what you are—you
can be vain and loud enough.

DORIMANT:

But not with so good a grace as Sir Fopling.—"Hey,
Hampshire!"—Oh, that sound! That sound becomes the mouth
of a man of quality.

MRS. LOVEIT:

Is there a thing so hateful as a senseless mimic?

DORIMANT:

He's a great grievance, indeed, to all who—like yourself, madam—love to play the fool in quiet.

MRS. LOVEIT:

A ridiculous animal, who has more of the ape than the ape has of the man in him.

DORIMANT:

I have as mean an opinion of a sheer mimic as yourself; yet were he all ape, I should prefer him to the gay, the giddy, brisk, insipid, noisy fool you dote on.

MRS. LOVEIT:

Those noisy fools, however you despise 'em, have good qualities which weigh more (or ought, at least) with us women than all the pernicious wit you have to boast of.

DORIMANT:

That I may hereafter have a just value for their merit, pray do me the favour to name 'em.

MRS. LOVEIT:

You'll despise 'em as the dull effects of ignorance and vanity, yet I care not if I mention some. First, they really do admire us, while you at best but flatter us well.

DORIMANT:

Take heed!—fools can dissemble too.

MRS. LOVEIT:

They may—but not so artificially as you. There is no fear they should deceive us. Then, they are assiduous, sir. They are ever offering us their service and always waiting on our will.

DORIMANT:

You owe that to their excessive idleness. They know not how to entertain themselves at home, and find so little welcome abroad, they are fain to fly to you who countenance 'em, as a refuge against the solitude they would be otherwise condemned to.

MRS. LOVEIT:

Their conversation, too, diverts us better.

DORIMANT:

Playing with your fan, smelling to your gloves, commending your hair, and taking notice how 'tis cut and shaded after the new way—

MRS. LOVEIT:

Were it any sillier than you can make it, you must allow 'tis pleasanter to laugh at others than to be laughed at ourselves, though never so wittily. Then, though they want skill to flatter us, they flatter themselves so well, they save us the labour. We need not take that care and pains to satisfy 'em of our love, which we so often lose on you.

DORIMANT:

They commonly, indeed, believe too well of themselves, and always better of you than you deserve.

MRS. LOVEIT:

You are in the right: they have an implicit faith in us, which keeps 'em from prying narrowly into our secrets, and saves us the vexatious trouble of clearing doubts which your subtle and causeless jealousies every moment raise.

DORIMANT:

There is an inbred falsehood in women which inclines 'em still to them whom they may most easily deceive.

MRS. LOVEIT:

The man who loves above his quality does not suffer more from the insolent impertinence of his mistress than the woman who loves above her understanding does from the arrogant presumptions of her friend.

DORIMANT:

You mistake the use of fools: they are designed for properties and not for friends. You have an indifferent stock of reputation left yet. Lose it all like a frank gamester on the square. 'Twill then be time enough to turn rook and cheat it up again on a good, substantial bubble.

MRS. LOVEIT:

The old and ill-favoured are only fit for properties, indeed, but young and handsome fools have met with kinder fortunes.

DORIMANT:

They have, to the shame of your sex be it spoken. 'Twas this, the thought of this, made me by a timely jealousy endeavour to prevent the good fortune you are providing for Sir Fopling. But against a woman's frailty all our care is vain.

MRS. LOVEIT:

Had I not with the dear experience bought the knowledge of your falsehood, you might have fooled me yet. This is not the first jealousy you have feigned to make a quarrel with me, and get a week to throw away on some such unknown, inconsiderable slut as you have been lately lurking with at plays.

DORIMANT:

Women, when they would break off with a man, never want the address to turn the fault on him.

MRS. LOVEIT:

You take a pride of late in using of me ill, that the town may know the power you have over me, which now (as unreasonably as yourself) expects that I, do me all the injuries you can, must love you still.

DORIMANT:

I am so far from expecting that you should, I begin to think you never did love me.

MRS. LOVEIT:

Would the memory of it were so wholly worn out in me that I did doubt it too. What made you come to disturb my growing quiet?

DORIMANT:

To give you joy of your growing infamy.

MRS. LOVEIT:

Insupportable! Insulting devil! This from you, the only author of my shame! This from another had been but justice, but from you, 'tis a hellish and inhuman outrage. What have I done?

DORIMANT:

A thing that puts you below my scorn and makes my anger as ridiculous as you have made my love.

MRS. LOVEIT:

I walked last night with Sir Fopling.

DORIMANT:

You did, madam; and you talked and laughed aloud, "Ha, ha, ha." Oh, that laugh! That laugh becomes the confidence of a woman of quality.

MRS. LOVEIT:

You, who have more pleasure in the ruin of a woman's reputation than in the endearments of her love, reproach me not with yourself—and I defy you to name the man can lay a blemish on my fame.

DORIMANT:

To be seen publicly so transported with the vain follies of that notorious fop, to me is an infamy below the sin of prostitution with another man.

MRS. LOVEIT:

Rail on! I am satisfied in the justice of what I did: you had pro-
voked me to it.

DORIMANT:

What I did was the effect of a passion whose extravagancies you
have been willing to forgive.

MRS. LOVEIT:

And what I did was the effect of a passion you may forgive it
you think fit.

DORIMANT:

Are you so indifferent grown?

MRS. LOVEIT:

I am.

DORIMANT:

Nay, then 'tis time to part. I'll send you back your letters you
have so often asked for. (*Looks in his pockets.*) I have two or three
of 'em about me.

MRS. LOVEIT:

Give 'em me.

DORIMANT:

You snatch as if you thought I would not. (*Gives her the letters.*)—
There. And may the perjuries in 'em be mine if e'er I see you
more. (*Offers to go: she catches him.*)

MRS. LOVEIT:

Stay!

DORIMANT:

I will not.

MRS. LOVEIT:

You shall!

DORIMANT:

What have you to say?

MRS. LOVEIT:

I cannot speak it yet.

DORIMANT:

Something more in commendation of the fool. Death, I want patience! Let me go.

MRS. LOVEIT:

I cannot. (*Aside.*) I can sooner part with the limbs that hold
him.—I hate that nauseous fool, you know I do.

DORIMANT:

Was it the scandal you were fond of, then?

MRS. LOVEIT:

You had raised my anger equal to my love, a thing you ne'er could do before; and in revenge I did—I know not what I did. Would you would not think on't any more.

DORIMANT:

Should I be willing to forget it, I shall be daily minded of it. 'Twill be a commonplace for all the town to laugh at me, and Medley, when he is rhetorically drunk, will ever be declaiming on it in my ears.

MRS. LOVEIT:

'Twill be believed a jealous spite! Come, forget it.

DORIMANT:

Let me consult my reputation; you are too careless of it. (*Pauses.*) You shall meet Sir Fopling in the Mall again tonight.

MRS. LOVEIT:

What mean you?

DORIMANT:

I have thought on it and you must. 'Tis necessary to justify my love to the world. You can handle a coxcomb as he deserves when you are not out of humour, madam.

MRS. LOVEIT:

Public satisfaction for the wrong I have done you! This is some new device to make me more ridiculous.

DORIMANT:

Hear me.

MRS. LOVEIT:

I will not.

DORIMANT:

You will be persuaded.

MRS. LOVEIT:

Never!

DORIMANT:

Are you so obstinate?

MRS. LOVEIT:

Are you so base?

DORIMANT:

You will not satisfy my love?

MRS. LOVEIT:

I would die to satisfy that; but I will not, to save you from a thousand racks, do a shameless thing to please your vanity.

DORIMANT:

Farewell, false woman!

MRS. LOVEIT:

Do! Go!

DORIMANT:

You will call me back again.

MRS. LOVEIT:

Exquisite fiend! I knew you came but to torment me.

MARRIAGE A-LA-MODE

by John Dryden

Doralice
Palamede

From his arrival in Sicily at the start of the play, Palamede has pursued Doralice, the wife of his friend. During several meetings, Doralice has been coy, but has avoided any kind of tryst with Palamede. However, bored with her own marriage and knowing her own husband has as mistress the woman promised to Palamede, Doralice begins to encourage the advances of her new lover.

DORALICE:

'Tis a strange thing that no warning will serve your turn; and that no retirement will secure me from your impertinent addresses! Did not I tell you, that I was to be private here at my devotions?

PALAMEDE:

Yes; and you see I have observ'd my cue exactly: I am come to relieve you from them. Come, shut up, shut up your book; the man's come who is to supply all your necessities.

DORALICE:

Then, it seems, you are so impudent to think it was an assignation? this, I warrant, was your lewd interpretation of my innocent meaning.

PALAMEDE:

Venus forbid that I should harbour so unreasonable a thought of a fair young lady, that you should lead me hither into temptation. I confess I might think indeed it was a kind of honourable challenge, to meet privately without seconds, and decide the difference betwixt the two sexes; but heaven forgive me if I thought amiss.

DORALICE:

You thought too, I'll lay my life on't, that you might as well make love to me, as my husband does to your mistress.

PALAMEDE:

I was so unreasonable to think so too.

DORALICE:

And then you wickedly inferr'd, that there was some justice in the revenge of it: or at least but little injury; for a man to endeavour to enjoy that, which he accounts a blessing, and which is not valu'd as it ought by the dull possessour. Confess your wickedness, did you not think so?

PALAMEDE:

I confess I was thinking so, as fast as I could; but you think so much before me, that you will let me think nothing.

DORALICE:

'Tis the very thing that I design'd: I have forestall'd all your arguments, and left you without a word more, to plead for mercy. If you have anything farther to offer, ere sentence pass—Poor animal, I brought you hither only for my diversion.

PALAMEDE:

That you may have, if you'll make use of me the right way; but I tell thee, woman, I am now past talking.

DORALICE:

But it may be, I came hither to hear what fine things you could say for yourself.

PALAMEDE:

You would be very angry, to my knowledge, if I should lose so much time to say many of 'em.—By this hand you would.—

DORALICE:

Fie, Palamede, I am a woman of honour.

PALAMEDE:

I see you are; you have kept touch with your assignation: and before we part, you shall find that I am a man of honour:—yet I have one scruple of conscience—

DORALICE:

I warrant you will not want some naughty argument or other to satisfy yourself.—I hope you are afraid of betraying your friend?

PALAMEDE:

Of betraying my friend! I am more afraid of being betray'd by you to my friend. You women now are got into the way of telling first yourselves: a man who has any care of his reputation will be loath to trust it with you.

DORALICE:

O you charge your faults upon our sex: you men are like cocks, you never make love, but you clap your wings, and crow when you have done.

PALAMEDE:

Nay, rather you women are like hens; you never lay, but you cackle an hour after, to discover your nest.—But I'll venture it for once.

DORALICE:

To convince you that you are in the wrong, I'll retire into the dark grotto, to my devotion, and make so little noise, that it shall be impossible for you to find me.

PALAMEDE:

But if I find you—

DORALICE:

Ay, if you find me—But I'll put you to search in more corners than you imagine. (*She runs in, and he after her.*)

THE BEAUX' STRATAGEM ❧

by George Farquhar

Cherry
Archer

Cherry, the daughter of an innkeeper, is wooed by Archer, a rogue disguised as a manservant. She holds her own against the conniving young man, much to his surprise and delight.

CHERRY:

(*Aside.*) Gone! and Martin here! I hope he did not listen; I would have the merit of the discovery all my own, because I would oblige him to love me. Mr. Martin, who was that man with my father?

ARCHER:

Some recruiting sergeant or trooper flogged out of the Army, I suppose.

CHERRY:

(*Aside.*) All's safe, I find.

ARCHER:

Come, my dear, have you conned over the catechise I taught you last night?

CHERRY:

Come, question me.

ARCHER:

What is love?

CHERRY:

Love is I know not what, it comes I know not how, and goes I know not when.

ARCHER:

Very well, an apt scholar.—(*Chucks her under the chin.*) Where does love enter?

CHERRY:

Into the eyes.

ARCHER:

And where go out?

CHERRY:

I won't tell ye.

ARCHER:

What are the objects of that passion?

CHERRY:

Youth, beauty, and clean linen.

ARCHER:

The reason?

CHERRY:

The two first are fashionable in nature, and the third at court.

ARCHER:

That's my dear.—What are the signs and tokens of that passion?

CHERRY:

A stealing look, a stammering tongue, words improbable, designs impossible, and actions impracticable.

ARCHER:

That's my good child, kiss me.—What must a lover do to obtain his mistress?

CHERRY:

He must adore the person that disdains him, he must bribe the chambermaid that betrays him, and court the footman that laughs at him.—He must, he must—

ARCHER:

Nay, child, I must whip you if you don't mind your lesson; he must treat his—

CHERRY:

Oh, ay!—he must treat his enemies with respect, his friends with indifference, and all the world with contempt; he must suffer much, and fear more; he must desire much, and hope little; in short, he must embrace his ruin, and throw himself away.

ARCHER:

Had ever man so hopeful a pupil as mine! Come, my dear, why is love called a riddle?

CHERRY:

Because, being blind, he leads those that see, and, though a child, he governs a man.

ARCHER:

Mighty well!—And why is love pictured blind?

CHERRY:

Because the painters out of the weakness or privilege of their art chose to hide the those eyes that they could not draw.

ARCHER:

That's my dear little scholar, kiss me again.—And why should love, that's a child, govern a man?

CHERRY:

Because that a child is the end of love.

ARCHER:

And so ends love's catechism.—And now, my dear, we'll go in and make my master's bed.

CHERRY:

Hold, hold, Mr. Martin! You have taken a great deal of pains to instruct me, and what d'ye think I have learnt by it?

ARCHER:

What?

CHERRY:

That you discourse and your habit are contradictions, and it would be nonsense in me to believe you are a footman any longer.

ARCHER:

'Oons, what a witch it is!

CHERRY:

Depend upon this, sir, nothing in this garb shall ever tempt me; for, though I was born to servitude, I hate it. Own your condition, swear you love me, and then—

ARCHER:

And then we shall go make the bed?

CHERRY:

Yes.

ARCHER:

You must know, then, that I am born a gentleman, my education was liberal; but I went to London a younger brother, fell into the hands of sharpers, who stripped me of my money; my friends disowned me, and now my necessity brings me to what you see.

CHERRY:

Then take my hand—promise to marry me before you sleep, and I'll make you master of two thousand pound.

ARCHER:

How?

CHERRY:

Two thousand pound that I have this minute in my own custody; so, throw off your livery this instant, and I'll go find a parson.

ARCHER:

What said you? A parson!

CHERRY:

What! do you scruple?

ARCHER:

Scruple! no, no, but—Two thousand pound, you say?

CHERRY:

And better.

ARCHER:

(*Aside.*) 'Sdeath, what shall I do? (*Aloud.*) But hark'ee, child, what need you make me master of yourself and money, when you may have the same pleasure out of me, and still keep your fortune in your hands?

CHERRY:

Then you won't marry me?

ARCHER:

I would marry you, but—

CHERRY:

O sweet sir, I'm your humble servant! you're fairly caught: would you persuade me that any gentleman who could bear the scandal of wearing livery would refuse two thousand pound, let the condition be what it would? No, no, sir. But I hope you'll pardon the freedom I have taken, since it was only to inform myself of the respect that I ought to pay you. (*Going.*)

ARCHER:

(*Aside.*) Fairly bit, by Jupiter! Hold! hold! And have you actually two thousand pound?

CHERRY:

Sir, I have my secrets as well as you; when you please to be more open, I shall be more free, and be assured that I have discoveries that will match yours, be what they will—in the meanwhile, be satisfied that no discovery I make shall ever hurt you; but beware my father! (*Exit Cherry.*)

ARCHER:

So! we're like to have as many adventures in our inns as Don Quixote had in his. Let me see—two thousand pound! If the wench would promise to die when the money were spent, igad, one would marry her; but the fortune may go off in a year or two, and the wife may live—Lord knows how long. Then an

innkeeper's daughter! ay, that's the devil—there my pride
brings me off.
For whatsoe'er the sages charge on pride,
The angels' fall, and twenty faults beside,
On earth, I'm sure, 'mong us of mortal calling.
Pride saves man oft, and woman too, from falling. (*Exits.*)

VENICE PRESERVED; or, A PLOT DISCOVERED ✍

by Thomas Otway

Aquilina

Antonio

*In this play of corruption and tragedy, Aquilina, a Greek courte-
san in love with the rogue Pierre, is courted, to her dismay, by
Antonio, a villainous Senator. Aquilina tries to fend him off, as
does Pierre, but Antonio is relentless in his desires.*

ANTONIO:

Nacky, Nacky, Nacky—how dost do, Nacky? Hurry durry. I am
come, little Nacky; past eleven a-clock, a late hour; time in all
conscience to go to bed, Nacky—Nacky, did I say? Aye, Nacky;
Aquilina, lina, lina, quilina, quilina, quilina, Aquilina,
Naquilina, Naquilina, Acky, Acky, Nacky, Nacky, queen
Nacky—come, let's to bed—you fubbs, you pugg, you—you little puss—purree tuzzey—I am a senator.

AQUILINA:

You are a fool, I am sure.

ANTONIO:

May be so, too sweetheart. Never the worse senator for all that.
Come Nacky, Nacky, let's have a game at rump, Nacky.

AQUILINA:

You would do well, signior, to be troublesome here no longer,
but leave me to myself, be sober and go home, sir.

ANTONIO:

Home, Madonna!

AQUILINA:

Aye, home, sir. Who am I?

ANTONIO:

Madonna, as I take it you are my—you are—thou art my little
Nicky Nacky—that's all!

AQUILINA:

I find you are resolved to be troublesome; and so to make short
of the matter in few words, I hate you, detest you, loathe you, I

am weary of you, sick of you—hang you, you are an old, silly, impertinent, impotent, solicitous coxcomb, crazy in your head and lazy in your body, love to be meddling with everything, and if you had not money, you are good for nothing.

ANTONIO:

Good for nothing! Hurry durry, I'll try that presently. Sixty-one years old and good for nothing; that's brave! "Good for nothing you say."

AQUILINA:

Why, what are you good for?

ANTONIO:

In the first place, madam, I am old, and consequently, very wise, very wise, Madonna, d'e mark that? In the second place, take notice, if you please, that I am a senator, and when I think fit can make speeches, Madonna. Hurry durry, I can make a speech in the Senate house now and then—would make your hair stand on end, Madonna.

AQUILINA:

What care I for your speeches in the Senate-house? If you would be silent here, I should thank you.

ANTONIO:

Why, I can make speeches to thee, too, my lovely Madonna; for example: "My cruel fair one (*Takes out a purse of gold and at every pause shakes it.*) since it is my fate that you should with your servant angry prove; though late at night—I hope 'tis not too late with this to gain reception for my love."—There's for thee, my little Nicky Nacky—take it, here take it—I say take it, or I'll throw it at your head. How now, rebel!

AQUILINA:

Truly, my illustrious senator, I must confess your honor is at present most profoundly eloquent, indeed!

ANTONIO:

Very well: come now, let's sit down and think upon't a little. Come sit, I say—sit down by me a little, my Nicky Nacky, hah— (*Sits down.*) Hurry durry—"good for nothing!"

AQUILINA:

No, sir; if you please, I can know my distance and stand.

ANTONIO:

Stand! How? Nacky up, and I down! Nay, then, let me exclaim with the poet,

Show me a case more pitiful who can,

A standing woman, and a falling man.

Hurry durry—not sit down! See this, ye gods.—You won't sit down?

 AQUILINA:

No, sir.

ANTONIO:

Then look you now, suppose me a bull, a Basan-bull, the bull of bulls, or any bull. Thus up I get and with my brows thus bent—I broo, I say I broo, I broo, I broo. You won't sit down, will you? I broo—(*Bellows like a bull, and drives her about.*)

AQUILINA:

Well, sir, I must endure this. (*She sits down.*) Now your honor has been a bull, pray what beast will your worship please to be next?

ANTONIO:

Now I'll be a senator again, and thy lover, little Nicky Nacky! (*He sits by her.*) Ah, toad, toad, toad, toad! spit in my face a little, Nacky—spit in my face, prithee, spit in my face, never so little. Spit but a little bit—spit, spit, spit, spit when you are bid, I say; do, prithee, spit—now, now, now, spit. What, you won't spit, will you? Then I'll be a dog.

AQUILINA:

A dog, my lord?

ANTONIO:

Aye, a dog,—and I'll give thee this t'other purse to let me be a dog—and to use me like a dog a little. Hurry durry—I will—here 'tis. (*Gives the purse.*)

AQUILINA:

Well, with all my heart. But let me beseech your dogship to play your tricks over as fast as you can, that you may come to stinking the sooner and be turned out of doors as you deserve.

ANTONIO:

Aye, aye—no matter for that—that shant' move me. (*He gets under the table.*) Now, bough, waugh waugh, bough waugh (*Barks like a dog.*)

AQUILINA:

Hold, hold, hold, sir, I beseech you: what is't you do? If curs bite, they must be kicked, sir. Do you see, kicked thus?

ANTONIO:

Aye, with all my heart. Do kick, kick on; now I am under the
table, kick again—kick harder, harder yet, bough waugh waugh
waugh, bough—'odd, I'll have a snap at thy shins—bough
waugh wough, waugh, bough! 'Odd, she kicks bravely.

AQUILINA:

Nay, then, I'll go another way to work with you; and I think
here's an instrument fit for the purpose. (*Fetches a whip and bell.*)
What, bite your mistress, sirrah! out, out of doors, you dog, to
kennel and be hanged—bite your mistress by the legs, you
rogue! (*She whips him.*)

ANTONIO:

Nay, prithee, Nacky, now thou art too loving! Hurry durry,
'odd! I'll be a dog no longer.

AQUILINA:

Nay, none of your fawning and grinning, but begone, or here's
the discipline! What, bite your mistress by the legs, you mon-
grel? Out of doors—hout hout, to kennel, sirrah! go!

ANTONIO:

This is very barbarous usage, Nacky, very barbarous. Look you,
I will not go—I will not stir from the door; that I resolve—hurry
durry, what shut me out? (*She whips him out.*)

AQUILINA:

Aye, and if you come here anymore tonight, I'll have my foot-
men lug you, you cur. What, bite your poor mistress Nacky, sirrah?

THE BEAUX' STRATAGEM ✎

by George Farquhar

Mrs. Sullen
Archer

Mrs. Sullen, caught in a loveless marriage to a loathsome man, discovers an outlet for her frustrations in Archer, a rogue disguised as a manservant to Aimwell. Mrs. Sullen's desires for escape come true when Archer visits her in her room.

MRS. SULLEN:

Thoughts free! are they so? Why, then suppose him here, dressed like a youthful, gay and burning bridegroom (*Archer steals out of the closet.*), with tongue enchanting, eyes bewitching, knees imploring (*Turns a little o' one side and sees Archer in the posture she describes.*)—ah! (*Shrieks, and runs to the other side of the stage.*) Have my thoughts raised a spirit? What are you, sir, a man or a devil?

ARCHER:

(*Rising.*) A man, a man, madam.

MRS. SULLEN:

How shall I be sure of it?

ARCHER:

Madam, I'll give you a demonstration this minute. (*Takes her hand.*)

MRS. SULLEN:

What, sir! do you intend to be rude?

ARCHER:

Yes, madam, if you please.

MRS. SULLEN:

In the name of wonder, whence came ye?

ARCHER:

From the skies, madam—I'm a Jupiter in love.

MRS. SULLEN:

How came you in?

ARCHER:

I flew in at the window, madam; your cousin Cupid lent me his wings, and your sister Venus opened the casement.

MRS. SULLEN:

I'm struck dumb with admiration.

ARCHER:

And I—with wonder! (*Looks passionately at her.*)

MRS. SULLEN:

What will become of me?

ARCHER:

How beautiful she looks!

Lilies unfold their white, their fragrant charms,

When the warm sun thus darts into their arms. (*Runs to her.*)

MRS. SULLEN:

(*Shrieks.*) Ah!

ARCHER:

'Oons, madam, what d'ye mean? you'll raise the house.

MRS. SULLEN:

Sir, I'll wake the dead before I bear this!—What! approach me with the freedoms of a keeper! I'm glad on't your impudence has cured me.

ARCHER:

If this be impudence (*Kneels.*) I leave to your partial self; no panting pilgrim, after a tedious, painful voyage, e'er bowed before his saint with more devotion.

MRS. SULLEN:

(*Aside.*) Now, now, I'm ruined if he kneels—Rise, thou prostrate engineer, not all thy undermining skill shall reach my heart. Rise, and know I can love to all the tenderness of wishes, sighs and tears—but go no farther. Still, to convince you that I'm more than woman, I can speak my frailty, confess my weakness even for you—but—

ARCHER:

(*Going to lay hold on her.*) For me!

MRS. SULLEN:

Hold, sir! build not upon that; for my most mortal hatred follows if you disobey what I command you now. Leave me this minute.—(*Aside.*) If he denies, I'm lost.

ARCHER:

Then you'll promise—

MRS. SULLEN:

Anything another time.

ARCHER:

When shall I come?

MRS. SULLEN:

Tomorrow when you will.

ARCHER:

Your lips must seal the promise.

MRS. SULLEN:

Pshaw!

ARCHER:

They must! they must! (*Kisses her.*) Raptures and paradise!—
And why not now, my angel? the time, the place, silence, and
secrecy, all conspire. And the now conscious stars have preor-
dained this moment for my happiness. (*Takes her in his arms.*)

MRS. SULLEN:

You will not! cannot, sure!

ARCHER:

If the sun rides fast, and disappoints not mortals of tomorrow's
dawn, this night shall crown my joys.

MRS. SULLEN:

My sex's pride assist me!

ARCHER:

My sex's strength help me!

MRS. SULLEN:

You shall kill me first!

ARCHER:

I'll die with you! (*Carrying her off.*)

MRS. SULLEN:

Thieves! thieves! murder!

THE RELAPSE 🪶
by John VanBrugh

Loveless
Amanda

Loveless, a gentleman married to Amanda, has seen a beautiful woman with whom he has fallen in love. Not knowing the woman was Berinthea, Amanda's cousin, Loveless tells Amanda of his encounter.

LOVELESS:
How do you like these lodgings, my dear? For my part, I am so well pleased with 'em, I shall hardly remove whilst we stay in town, if you are satisfied.

AMANDA:
I am satisfied with everything that pleases you; else I had not come to town at all.

LOVELESS:
Oh, a little of the noise and bustle of the world sweetens the pleasures of retreat: we shall find the charms of our retirement doubled, when we return to it.

AMANDA:
That pleasing prospect will be my chiefest entertainment, whilst (much against my will) I am obliged to stand surrounded with these empty pleasures which 'tis so much the fashion to be fond of.

LOVELESS:
I own most of 'em are indeed but empty; nay, so empty, that one would wonder by what magic power they act, when they induce us to be vicious for their sakes. Yet some there are we may speak kindlier of: there are delights, of which a private life is destitute, which may divert an honest man, and be a harmless entertainment to a virtuous woman. The conversation of the town is one; and truly (with some small allowances) the plays, I think, may be esteemed another.

AMANDA:
The plays, I must confess, have some small charms, and would

have more, would they restrain that loose, obscene encouragement to vice which shocks, if not the virtue of some women, at least the modesty of all.

LOVELESS:

But till that reformation can be made I would not leave the wholesome corn for some intruding tares that grow amongst it. Doubtless the moral of a well-wrought scene is of prevailing force—last night there happened one that moved me strangely.

AMANDA:

Pray, what was that?

LOVELESS:

Why, 'twas about—but 'tis not worth repeating.

AMANDA:

Yes, pray let me know it.

LOVELESS:

No, I think 'tis as well let alone.

AMANDA:

Nay, now you make me have a mind to know.

LOVELESS:

'Twas a foolish thing: you'd perhaps grow jealous should I tell it you, though without cause, heaven knows.

AMANDA:

I shall begin to think I have a cause, if you persist in making it a secret.

LOVELESS:

I'll then convince you you have none, by making it no longer so. Know then, I happened in the play to find my very character, only with the addition of a relapse, which struck me so, I put a sudden stop to a most harmless entertainment which till then diverted me between the acts. 'Twas to admire the workmanship of nature in the face of a young lady that sat some distance from me, she was so exquisitely handsome.

AMANDA:

"So exquisitely handsome!"

LOVELESS:

Why do you repeat my words, my dear?

AMANDA:

Because you seemed to speak 'em with such pleasure, I though I might oblige you with their echo.

LOVELESS:

Then you are alarmed, Amanda?

AMANDA:

It is my duty to be so, when you are in danger.

LOVELESS:

You are too quick in apprehending for me; all will be well when you have heard me out. I do confess I gazed upon her, nay, eagerly I gazed upon her.

AMANDA:

Eagerly? That's with desire.

LOVELESS:

No, I desired her not: I viewed her with a world of admiration, but no one glance of love.

AMANDA:

Take heed of trusting to such nice distinctions.

LOVELESS:

I did take heed; for, observing in the play that he who seemed to represent me there was, by an accident like this, unwarily surprised into a net in which he lay a poor entangled slave, and brought a train of mischiefs on his head, I snatched my eyes away; they pleaded hard for leave to look again, so but I grew absolute, and they obeyed.

AMANDA:

Were they the only things that were inquisitive? Had I been in your place, my tongue, I fancy, had been curious, too: I should have asked her name, and where she lived (yet still without design). Who was she, pray?

LOVELESS:

Indeed I cannot tell.

AMANDA:

You will not tell.

LOVELESS:

By all that's sacred, then, I did not ask.

AMANDA:

Nor do you know what company was with her?

LOVELESS:

I do not.

AMANDA:

Then I am calm again.

LOVELESS:

Why were you disturbed?

AMANDA:

Had I then no cause?

LOVELESS:

None, certainly.

AMANDA:

I thought I had.

LOVELESS:

But you thought wrong, Amanda; for turn the case, and let it be your story. Should you come home, and tell me you had seen a handsome man, should I grow jealous because you had eyes?

AMANDA:

But should I tell you he were exquisitely so; that I had gazed on him with admiration; that I had looked with eager eyes upon him; should you not think 'twere possible I might go one step farther, and enquire his name?

LOVELESS:

(*Aside.*) She has reason on her side: I have talked too much; but I must turn it off another way. (*To Amanda.*) Will you then make no difference, Amanda, between the language of our sex and yours? There is a modesty restrains your tongues which makes you speak by halves when you commend; but roving flattery gives a loose to ours, which makes us still speak double what we think: you should not therefore in so strict a sense take what I said to her advantage.

AMANDA:

Those flights of flattery, sir, are to our faces only: when women once are out of hearing, you are as modest in your commendations as we are. But I shan't put you to the trouble of farther excuses; if you please, this business shall rest here. Only give me leave to wish, both for your peace and mine, that you may never meet this miracle of beauty more.

LOVELESS:

I am content.

SOURCES ✍

Complete Texts of the Plays Excerpted
as Monologues and Scenes in this Volume

Addison, Joeseph. *The Drummer*, Vol. XI of *Bell's British Theatre 1776-1781*. Gen. Ed. Byrne R.S. Fone. New York: AMS, Inc., 1977.

Behn, Aphra. *The Works of Aphra Behn*. (6 vols.) Ed. Montague Summer. New York: Benjamin Blom, 1967.

Centlivre, Susanna. *To Wonder: A Woman Keeps a Secret*, Vol. IV of *Bell's British Theatre 1776-1781*. Gen. Ed. Byrne R.S. Fone. New York: AMS, Inc., 1977.

Cibber, Colley. *The Careless Husband*, in *Restoration Comedy*. Ed. Alexander Jeffares. New Jersey: Rowman Littlefield, 1974.

Cibber, Colley. *Love's Last Shift*, Vol. VIII of *Bell's British Theatre 1776-1781*. Gen. Ed. Byrne R. S. Fone. New York: AMS, Inc., 1977.

Cibber, Colley. *The Refusal*, Vol. XI of *Bell's British Theatre 1776-1781*. Gen. Ed. Bryne R. S. Fone. New York: AMS, Inc., 1977.

Cibber, Colley. *She Would and She Would Not*, Vol. VI of *Bell's British Theatre 1776-1781*. Gen. Ed. Byrne R.S. Fone. New York: AMS, Inc., 1977.

Congreve, William. *The Complete Plays of William Congreve*. Ed. Herbert Davis. Chicago: University of Chicago Press, 1967.

Dryden, John. *John Dryden: Four Comedies*. Ed. L. A. Beaurline and Fredson Bowers. Chicago: The University of Chicago Press, 1967.

Etherege, George. *The Plays of George Etherege*. Ed. Michael Cordner. Cambridge: Cambridge University Press, 1982.

Farquhar, George. *The Works of George Farquhar* (2 vol.). Ed. Shirley Strum Kenny. Oxford: Clarendon Press, 1988.

Johnson, Charles. *The Country Lasses*, Vol. XIX of *Bell's British Theatre 1776-1781*. Gen. Ed. Byrne R.S. Fone. New York: AMS, Inc., 1977.

Otway, Thomas. *Venice Preserved*. Ed. Malcolm Kelsall. Lincoln: University of Nebraska Press, 1969.

Southerne, Thomas. *The Works of Thomas Southerne (2 vol.)*. Ed. Robert Jordan and Harold Love. Oxford: Clarendon Press, 1988.

VanBrugh, John *The Complete Works of Sir John VanBrugh*. Plays Ed. Bonamy Dobree. New York: AMS Press, Inc., 1967.

Villiers, George. *The Rehearsal*, Vol. XV of *Bell's British Theatre 1776-1781*, Gen. Ed. Byrne R. S. Fone. New York: AMS, Inc. 1977.

Wycherly, William. *The Plays of William Wycherly*. Ed. Peter Holland. Cambridge: Cambridge University Press, 1981.

SELECTED BIBLIOGRAPHY

RESTORATION THEATRE AND HISTORY

Anthony, Sister Rose, S.C. *The Jeremy Collier Stage Controversy 1698-1726.* New York: Benjamin Blom, 1966.

Aubrey's Brief Lives. London: Secker and Warbury, 1949.

Bliss, Robert M. *Restoration England 1660-1688.* London: Methuen, 1985.

Carlton, Charles. *Royal Mistresses.* London: Routledge, 1990.

Cibber, Colley. *An Apology for the Life of Mr. Colley Cibber,* edited by Robert W. Lowe, 2 vols. 1889; rpt. New York: AMS Press, 1966.

Clark, Andrew, ed. *'Brief Lives' chiefly of Contemporaries, set down by John Aubrey between the Years 1669 and 1696.* Oxford: Clarendon Press, 1898.

Fone, Byrne, RS, ed. *Bell's British Theatre.* New York: AMS Press, 1977.

Fraser, Antonia. *Royal Charles: Charles II and the Restoration.* New York: Alfred A. Knopf, 1979.

—. *The Weaker Vessel.* New York: Vintage Books, 1984

Greene, Graham. *Lord Rochester's Monkey.* New York: Penguin Books, Inc., 1974.

Highfill, Philip H., Jr., Kalman A. Burnim, and Edward A. Langhans, *A Biographical Dictionary of Actors, Actresses, Musicians, Dancers, Managers, and Other Stage Personnel in London, 1660-1800,* 16 vols., Carbondale: Southern Illinois University Press, 1992.

Howe, Elizabeth. *The First English Actresses: Women and Drama, 1660-1700.* Cambridge: Cambridge University Press, 1992.

Hume, Robert D., ed. *The London Theatre World 1660-1800*. Carbondale: Southern Illinois University Press, 1980.

Hutton, Ronald. *The Restoration: A Political and Religious History of England and Wales 1658-1667*. Oxford: Oxford University Press, 1985.

Kenyon, J.P. *Stuart England* (Second Edition). London: Penguin Books, 1978.

—. *The Stuarts: A Study in English Kingship*. New York: MacMillan Company, 1959.

Latham, Robert, ed. *The Illustrated Pepys: Extracts from the Diary*. Berkeley: University of California Press, 1978.

Loftis, John, Richard Southern, Marton Jones, and A.H. Scouten. *The Revels: History of Drama in English* (Volume V). London: Methuen, 1976.

Lucas-Dubreton, J. *Samuel Pepys - A Portrait in Miniature*. New York: G.P. Putnam's Sons, 1925.

McCollum, John I. Jr., ed. *The Restoration Stage*. Westport: Greenwood Press, 1973.

Milhous, Judith, and Robert D. Hume. *Producible Interpretation: Eight English Plays, 1675-1707*. Carbondale: Southern Illinois University Press, 1985.

Morgan, Fidelis. *The Female Wits: Women Playwrights on the London Stage, 1660-1720*. London: Virago Press Ltd., 1981.

Morgan, Kenneth O. *The Oxford Illustrated History of Britain*. Oxford: Oxford University Press, 1984.

Nettleton, George H. and Arthur E. Case, eds. *British Dramatists from Dryden to Sheridan*. Carbondale: Southern Illinois University Press, 1969.

Perry, Graham. *The Seventeeth Century – The Intellectual and Cultural Context of English Literature, 1603-1700*. London: Longman, 1989.

Roberts, David. *The Ladies: Female Patronage of Restoration Drama 1660-1700*. Oxford: Clarendon Press, 1989.

Rothstein, Eric. *George Farquhar*. New York: Twayne Publisher, 1967.

Schofield, Mary Anne and Cecelia Macheski, eds. *Curtain Calls: British and American Women and the Theatre 1660-1820*. Athens: Ohio University Press, 1991.

Stackhouse, Thomas, ed./ab. *Bishop Gilbert Burnett: History of His Own Time*. London: Guernsey Press, 1979.

Stone, Lawrence. *Road to Divorce: England 1530-1987*. Oxford: Oxford University Press, 1990.

Styan, J.L. *Restoration Comedy in Performance*. Cambridge: Cambridge University Press, 1986.

Summers, Montague. *The Playhouse of Pepys*. New York: Humanities Press, 1964.

Swain, A.E.H., ed. *Sir John VanBrugh*. New York: A.A. Wyn, Inc., 1949.

Thomas, David and Arnold Hare. *Restoration and Georgian England 1660-1788*. Cambridge: Cambridge University Press, 1989.

Wilson, John Harold. *All the King's Ladies: Actresses of the Restoration*. Chicago: University of Chicago Press, 1958.

Winn, James Anderson. *John Dryden and His World*. New Haven: Yale University Press, 1987.